# Rebuilding the Church

*Cover:*
St. Thomas' Anglican Church, St. Catharines, Ontario, Canada.
see page110

# Rebuilding
*the*
# Church
*on a new foundation*

GERALD ROBINSON

*with a Foreword by Herbert O'Driscoll*

WIPF & STOCK · Eugene Oregon

REBUILDING THE CHURCH ON A NEW FOUNDATION

Copyright © 2019 Gerald Robinson. All rights reserved. Except for brief quotations in critical publications or reviews, no part of this book may be reproduced in any manner without prior written permission from the publisher. Write: Permissions, Wipf and Stock Publishers, 199 W. 8th Ave., Suite 3, Eugene, OR 97401.

Wipf & Stock
An Imprint of Wipf and Stock Publishers
199 W. 8th Ave., Suite 3
Eugene, OR 97401

www.wipfandstock.com

PAPERBACK ISBN: 978-1-5326-7636-9
HARDCOVER ISBN: 978-1-5326-7637-6
EBOOK ISBN: 978-1-5326-7638-3

Manufactured in the U.S.A.

# Contents

Foreword by Herbert O'Driscoll     vii

**Building a New Foundation**

    Chapter 1: The Six Plans of Rudolf Schwarz     1

    Chapter 2: The Meaning of Space     12

    Chapter 3: The Anatomy of Worship     32

    Chapter 4: The Great Concordance     51

**Churches built with the Six Plans**

    Chapter 5: Examples of the First Plan     69

    Chapter 6: Examples of the Second Plan     90

    Chapter 7: Examples of the Third Plan     105

    Chapter 8: Examples of the Fourth Plan     131

    Chapter 9: Examples of the Fifth Plan     151

    Chapter 10: Examples of the Sixth Plan     171

**Support for the Gathering**

    Chapter 11: Supporting the Community     186

    Chapter 12: Supporting the Eucharist     198

    Chapter 13: Supporting the Word     206

    Chapter 14: Supporting Baptism     217

Photo Credits     222

Appendices     223

Bibliography     226

Index     228

# Foreword

These pages are designed to be first of all practical. They are for men and women who are setting out at the beginning of the twenty-first century to design and build a place for the worship of God. At first sight that may seem a simple task for which there is a vast and varied precedent. We have only to go about the task to realize that it offers a profound challenge.

If it be true that form follows function, what are we to do in the designing of sacred space when the function, that of worship, is a many-faceted mystery? Worship is a jewel that turns unceasingly, offering now this color and now that, responding now to this aspect of the human-divine encounter and now that. We need to ask countless questions of our needs as a worshiping community, our intentions as we set out to build, the way we have come to this point in our history, what the overriding symbols of our tradition may be, what modes of worship and gathering we may need. In what ways do we fashion a space for prayer, praise, music, silence, meditation, social gathering, reflection, study, the celebration of the events in human life—(the list is far from complete)?

We must go even further nowadays. We must acknowledge the fact that we live in immense change. The role of a Christian community may change with the changing community around it. The role and function of all institutional religion is being transformed by a changing relationship with society. Our very concepts of God are in transition as our relationship with creation itself moves towards possibilities both thrilling and fearful. All of these things are of significance when we set out to form a sacred space. We cannot say what will await the settling down of this immense transition we are in. In fact it is our awe before that transition process which calls more and more men and women to worship! Even in the wilderness it is most human to build the cairn, to erect the tent, to light the sacred fire, all the time telling the story which gives meaning to the wilderness journey and gives people the energy to continue.

This book is not a map but rather a compass. A map gives us detailed instructions, a compass points us in certain directions. A compass allows us greater freedom and thereby, of course, calls us to greater responsibility and to the need for using our creativity. These pages will give us a spectrum of choice. The choices are not so numerous as to make us despair. Rather, they are great and timeless shapes, each in a mysterious way both physical and spiritual. Each of the six will prove to have a great deal of freedom within its particular category. I suspect that the shape of the ultimate sacred space holds part of all these particular shapes, but then, in the presence of the Ultimate, all spaces will have become sacred. Perhaps that is why in the dream of John of Patmos, as he contemplates the Holy City he observes that there is no Temple in that city. The reason is that the City itself has become the Temple, thus becoming a fitting place in which the builder of both City and Temple may dwell.

Herbert O'Driscoll

Christ Church, Calgary, Alberta

# Chapter 1
# A New Foundation

This work was inspired by the writings of Rudolf Schwarz, a German architect and mystic who lived from 1897 to 1961. In 1938 Schwarz published his seminal work "Vom Bau der Kirche"[1] (from Building to Church). Schwarz proposed a system of ideas, what he called "The First Six Plans" that would embrace all the worship of the Christian Church. In those days it was extraordinary that Schwarz could record his tender insights into prayer and adoration at a time when the nation around him was being led by dark forces and entranced by manic visions of a destiny for its blood. Fear was being institutionalized, and religious rituals were being subverted to the glorification of the state and for an eternity that was to last for a millennium. It was extraordinary that in this hate-filled

FIGURE 1. Rudolf Schwarz 1897–1961

environment Schwarz could conduct his gentle enquiry into forms and spaces of worship, but somehow he survived; and after the war he was made responsible for the planning and rebuilding of the central area of the city of Cologne, this because he was one of the few German architects who had not been associated with the previous Nazi regime. Twenty years later, in 1958, an English translation of Schwarz's book titled "The

---

1. Schwarz, Rudolf, *Vom Bau der Kirche*, Heidelberg: Verlag Lambert Schneider, 1938.

Church Incarnate"[2] with a foreword by Mies van der Rohe was published. The Canadian Architect magazine received a review copy, and the editor, John Kettle, invited me to write the review. I had just arrived in Canada after graduating with a Master of Architecture degree from the Urban Design Studio at Harvard, but my real background was as a structural engineer which perhaps explains why I found the book so incredibly difficult to read. Its repetitive poetic style and elliptical imagery would send me to sleep, so at the end of a page I would have no memory of what I had just read. At the same time I felt there was something of real value in the book, something just out of reach. I phoned John Kettle to say I needed more time. I needed a lot more time; several years in fact. By the time I was able to write the review the book was out of print! It has taken me ten years to be able to read Schwarz's book, taking it a little at a time. It took ten more years to begin to have an understanding of it, and then, suddenly, after another ten years I was surprised to discover the work had great practical value. The insights I have gathered in my sixty-year association with Rudolf Schwarz have proved so valuable I am feeling an obligation to share them. I'm doing that in two volumes: a Companion[3] where I clarify his mystical wanderings, and this work which has the purpose of renewing the church by going back to its very beginnings; beginnings from which it may be reborn to survive into the next century.

Buildings enclose spaces, and Schwarz's approach was to observe the ways humans respond to the spaces they occupy. In particular he noted the ways in which a worshiping congregation is supported by its worship space. To formalize this he proposed a system of Six Plans that would embrace all their desires and wishes. These Six Plans were not building plans, they were vessels for ideas about space and worship—castles in the air. He cautioned against attempting to use them as designs for buildings, saying "The Plans are a happening that has withdrawn utterly into its potentiality, which has become wholly seed and beginning, and which waits, not to be copied, but to grow up once more as new" (and that is an example of his writing style.)

2. Schwarz, Rudolf, , *The Church Incarnate*, Translated by Cynthia Harris. Chicago: Henry Regnery, 1958.

3. Robinson, Gerald, *Sacred Journey, a Companion to Rudolf Schwarz's "The Church Incarnate"*. Eugene OR: Wipf & Stock, 2019.

## A New Foundation

Schwarz himself did not copy or use any of these Plans for any of the churches for which he was the Architect (with one exception which we will study in chapter 9). He was deeply religious, a conservative Catholic, so his planning was obedient to the doctrine of the day. His several churches in Germany are noted for their bold 1930s-Modern style. The interiors are elegant, almost austere, with lots of light from clear glass windows, but the people are confined to a traditional discipline of pews. They do not have the freedom to enjoy the other ways of gathering which he explored in his written works.

In his reflections Schwarz made several versions, sometimes incompatible versions, of each Plan; more than forty in total. These melt and merge into one another as in a dream landscape where he observes the reactions of a wandering congregation. To make this body of knowledge useful I have selected six Plans from this panoply; Plans whose spatial configurations support the worship of the six ministries of the Christian Church which I identify in chapter 3. I have expressed these Plans in the form of six new icons on the following two pages. These icons do not reproduce Schwarz's original diagrams but are compilations of features taken from several of his drawings. Also I have given new names to some of these new Plans, names which more usefully describe their qualities. These correspondences are listed in Appendix A.

Schwarz proposed spaces to serve the needs of a congregation, but his genius was to recognize that we are, in turn, influenced by the spaces we have chosen to occupy. To repeat a familiar quotation "We shape our buildings; and afterwards our buildings shape us."[4] Thus when we enter a space newly-designed for us we might be influenced by it to become a new people, and thereby have new needs which our "new" space is no longer able to satisfy. So Schwarz's listing of Six Plans becomes a progression where each Plan (which was developed to satisfy a need) creates a new awareness in the congregation. This could give rise to the congregation having new needs for which it would need a new Plan. The progression of ideas represented by Schwarz's Six Plans shows a progression from an introverted contemplative congregation to a confident outward-looking body. Schwarz created these Plans to reflect the aspirations of a worshiping people.

---

4. Winston Churchill, October 1943, in a speech debating the rebuilding of the House of Commons after its destruction by incendiary bombs during the war.

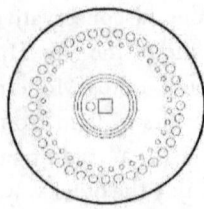

The First Plan, Sacred Inwardness, is in the form of an all-enclosing dome or igloo with strong solid walls and a central focus.

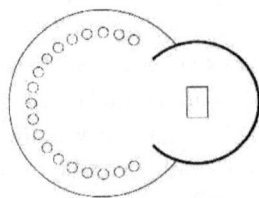

In the Second Plan, Sacred Meeting, part of the dome has become permeable to allow an awareness of the world, while keeping the interior safe, and permitting unimpeded access between the two areas.

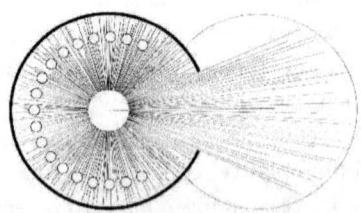

In the Third Plan, The Shining, the dome is breached, allowing light from the internal worship to shine out into the world.

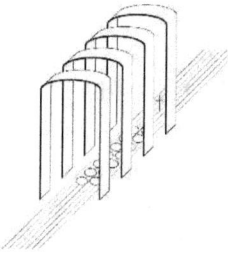

The Fourth Plan, Sacred Journey, is linear: an arching over an open-ended pilgrim way.

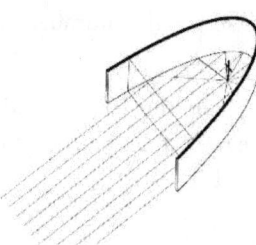

In the Fifth Plan, The Open Chalice, those on the Way are gathered into a welcoming enclosure.

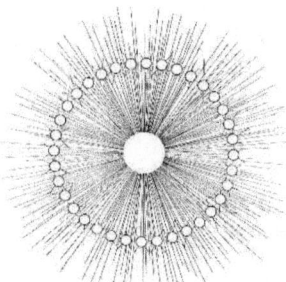

In the Sixth Plan, The Dome of Light, there are no solid walls. An outpouring of light illuminates the whole world.

Thus the Six Plans represent a gradual progression from an introspective contemplative worship to an extremely extroverted world view. Why are there just six? I don't know why, but I am sure it is the right number. In the fifth century St. Augustine of Hippo in his monumental "City of God" wrote:

> "The works of Creation are described as being repeated six times. The reason for this is that six is the number of perfection[5] ... it is the first number, as I have said, which is made up of the sum of its factors, and in this number God brought his works to complete perfection. Hence the theory of number is not to be lightly regarded since it is made quite clear in many passages of the Holy Scriptures how highly it is to be regarded ...
>
> "God, who could have created the world in an instant, instead chose to do it in six days, because six is the number of perfection."

The idea that a six-fold array could have universal significance also finds support from Confucius. In his Commentaries he notes that the word for family is made up from the characters for "six" and "relationship".

The six relationships that make up this concept are
1. father-to-son,
2. son-to-father,
3. husband-to-wife,
4. wife-to-husband,
5. elder brother-to-younger brother,
6. younger brother-to-elder brother.

These relationships can refer metaphorically to all social arrangements; as between cities, peoples, nations, societies, and their rulers. This is

---

5. Perfect numbers are those which are equal to the sum of their factors. Thus $1 \times 2 \times 3 = 6 = 1+2+3$. The next perfect number is 28, as $1+2+4+7+14 = 28$, followed by 496, 8128, 33,550,336 ... in a rapidly expanding infinite series, all of whose values end in a 6 or an 8.

another example where six relationships may be gathered together to form a coherent grouping.

The number six has an association with the process of creation as recorded in Genesis, and Schwarz carries this over into the process of creating spaces for Christian worship. In the next two chapters we will study space in the one, followed by worship in the other, and in a following chapter we will learn how they can be related.

I have illustrated Schwarz's progression of plans by a row of six icons with directional arrows between them.

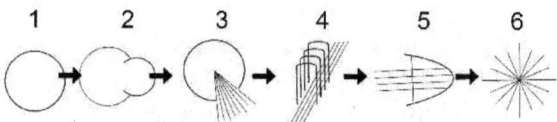

FIGURE 2. The Six Plans of Rudolf Schwarz showing a progression of development.

This works fine to illustrate the development of ideas, but not so well as a history of a real people. In that case the arrows would represent a vast migration of worshipers from the First Plan to the Second Plan, and so on. The outcome of this process would be for all the worshipers to finally end up in the Sixth Plan, leaving five empty churches in their wake. Obviously this is an unsatisfactory solution.

In an attempt to deal with this, Schwarz proposed in a following chapter what he calls The Seventh Plan. This Seventh Plan does not derive from the previous Sixth Plan. The contents page of his book shows that he places it in its own category, a sequel to the whole series of the Six— perhaps it would be better to have called it "Plan B" rather than "Plan 7". He gave this plan the grandiose title "The Cathedral of All Times (The Whole)"[6]. It consists of bits and pieces of all six of the previous Plans gathered together into a sort of a vast ecclesiastical department store where one may wander from ministry to ministry; church shopping.

I feel sympathy for Rudolf Schwarz being faced with this problem, but I cannot accept that what he proposed could be a practical solution because we humans are not able to live in All Times. We do not exist in

---

6. "Der Dom Aller Zeiten (Das Ganze)."

the whole of space, we occupy just a particular portion of it. Always we have lived and will live in a succession of particular Here's and Now's. That is the human condition, the context for our existence on Earth. Because his Cathedral of All Times (the Whole) is founded on a different premise from his Six Plans the so-called Seventh Plan cannot help us in creating a place of worship here on earth. Such a worship can exist only in the eternal timelessness of a space that is beyond space. Could this be his model for the worship of Heaven?

I see another possibility for resolving this dilemma, a solution which springs from Schwarz's illustration (figure 3) for the Sixth Plan, the Dome of Light. This shows the light shining out from the dome into all the world and the people going out into the world with the light—each person being a tiny spark of that great light, each person in his heart taking the light out into the world and being a tiny church.

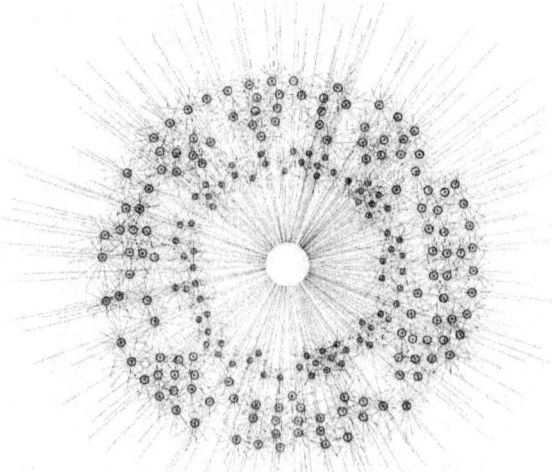

Figure 3. Rudolf Schwarz's illustration for the Dome of Light

If each individual spark of light becomes a new church what sort of church would that be? From Schwarz's beautiful illustration, taken from his German edition, we see the sparks are represented as tiny circles, tiny icons for the First Plan, so we see the Sixth Plan generating the First. If we accept this we can see a linkage between the Sixth Plan and the First Plan. The progression of Plans now becomes a Ring as shown in Figure 4, where successive Plans are linked by directional arrows. These arrows are not intended to indicate a migration of the people from one church to another—they illustrate an expanding of consciousness as the world turns.

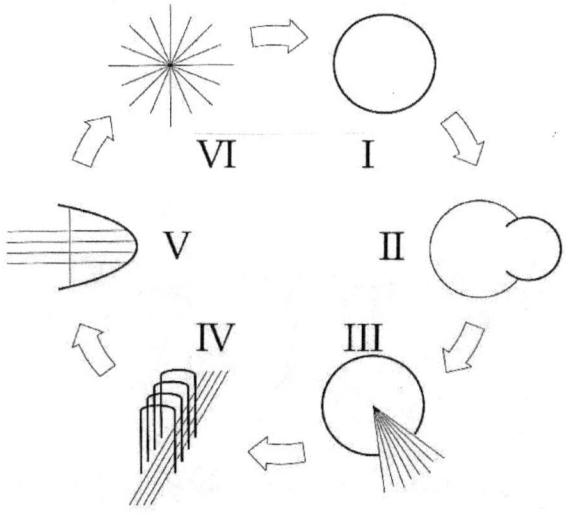

FIGURE 4. The Ring of Plans. The Sixth Plan generates the First Plan, completing the circle.

This rotation follows a progression found in the natural world (figure 5) where a buried seed, feeling the warmth of the sun, germinates and sends forth a shoot to bear a blossom which creates new seeds. Schwarz acknowledged this parallel, even though he did not illustrate it with a diagram, saying "We encountered this linking of forms into a logical sequence when we spoke about the growth of plants which brings forth one form after another and grows to fulfillment through a succession of phases." ... so perhaps he would approve.

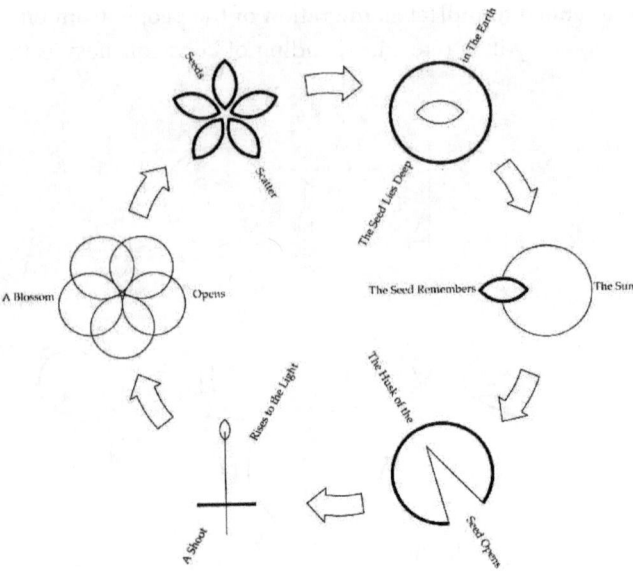

FIGURE 5. The Cycle of Nature. (Note the similarity of the icons to those in the previous illustration.)

**A Foundation for the Book**

I hope I have not done violence to Schwarz's listing of Six Plans by setting them in a cycle or ring. The value of this format is that later in the book we will see that the six ministries that constitute worship can also be set in a ring. This enables us to forge a six-fold unity between space and worship. but first we will need to configure these entities so they can be conjoined each with the other, and that is the purpose of the next two chapters: "The Meaning of Space" and "The Anatomy of Worship"; and these concepts are brought together in the chapter that follows them, titled "The Great Concordance".

Following this we have six chapters where we see twenty-four examples of existing churches, each of which has embodied one of the Six Plans into its built form. These churches are all very different from one another. They illustrate how the Six Plans are not formulae to be followed, but a new way of seeing.

Finally, there are four chapters titled "Support for the Gathering" in which we deal with the physical requirements for building a worship space that will serve a congregation. These chapters cover such items as layout, seating, access, lighting and acoustics. They show how a congregation, gathered into a worship space, could find fulfillment for its own special requirements.

**Summary of Chapter 1: A New Foundation**

1. The purpose of this work is to ensure the survival of the church into the next century. To achieve this the church needs rediscover its spiritual foundation.

2. In 1938 Rudolf Schwarz published a listing of six archetypal Plans. These were generated to create spaces that would satisfy the aspirations of their worshiping communities.

3. The First Plan, Sacred Inwardness, is in the form of an all-enclosing dome with strong solid walls.

4. In the Second Plan, Sacred Meeting, part of the dome has become permeable to allow an awareness of the world.

5. In the Third Plan, The Shining, the dome is breached, allowing light from the worship to shine out into the world.

6. The Fourth Plan, Sacred Journey, is linear: an arching over a path for a pilgrim community.

7. In the Fifth Plan, The Open Chalice, the Way is gathered up into a space of welcome.

8. In the Sixth Plan, The Dome of Light, the walls are transparent and allow an outpouring of light to illuminate the whole world.

9. These Plans may be arranged in a circle, as in Figure 4, to illustrate how each Plan has been generated to serve a human response to the previous one.

# Chapter 2
# The Meaning of Space

*Dictionaries define nets in terms of knots and bits of string.*
*It is the openings that catch the fish.*

**Making Space**

Dictionaries have a hard time with space. Either, as with prime numbers, they define space in terms of what it is not, or they use vague expansive words to define something vague and ethereal. Secretly, they know we know what space is. Perhaps they think we are only looking up the word to test them, but they feel obligated to give us some sort of a definition. They don't want to just leave a blank space; although that might serve as a good illustration.

The picture we build up from reading the many dictionary definitions of space is of a vague, formless, immaterial cloud; a sort of a hiatus between other definitions, and yet, space can inspire our emotions. Space can move us. Clearly something is missing here, missing from the dictionary definitions of space, something important.

There is a freedom in space. A bottle of Coke contains only Coke. An empty bottle, a bottle of space, can contain anything we like to put in it. Space is permissive. The optimist says the bottle is half full; the pessimist says it is half empty. For this to be valid we have to value whatever material thing is in the bottle. For those who make their own wine, empty bottles are at a premium. It is their emptiness, the space inside them, that makes them useful. From this perspective can we now begin to define space? Here is a preliminary listing of qualities which we will seek to flesh out in the following pages:

> Space is a potential for action.
> Space is nothing, waiting for something.
> Space is what was and is not, or what is yet to be.
> Space is feminine.
> Space is creative.
> Space is freedom.

Thinking in space-centered terms can give us a whole new perspective, one where we focus on our freedoms rather than on things that restrict us.

## The Usefulness of Space

Lao Tzu, a sixth-century-BC philosopher, asserts the usefulness of space[7] by considering a wheel, a cup, and a house.

> "Thirty spokes meet at the wheel's hub. It is the hole in the center that makes the wheel usable.
>
> "The potter forms clay into a cup. The hollow inside makes the cup useful.
>
> "Cut doors and windows to build a house. It is the interior space that is commodious.
>
> "Thus what is valuable is a function of what is; and what is useful is a function of what is not."

In a modern paraphrase we could say that when we build a house we pay for the walls, and when we rent a house we pay for the space. In relating this to architecture Amos Ih Tiao Chang[8] notes that it is the immaterial (the quality most likely to be overlooked) which is the most useful. The void, which conventionally is regarded as negative, is actually of greater importance, because it is always capable of being filled by something solid.

This resonates with a passage from the Letter to the Hebrews 11:1, 3 which also asserts the primacy of space:

> "Faith is the substance of things hoped for, the evidence of things not seen.
>
> "The World was created out of the void by faith.
>
> "Thus that which is seen was created out of that which is not seen."

---

6. Lao Tzu, *The Tao of Power*, 18.

7. Chang, *The Tao of Architecture*, 14.

Even the humble Coke bottle was created by breath out of the void, the Coke-bottle-shaped void into which a bubble of glass was blown.

**Positive Space**

We can visit and enjoy a city without entering any of the buildings. In fact we have to be outdoors to experience a city. We can experience food in a restaurant, music in a concert hall, but to experience a city we have to be in the park, in the square, on the street. So the art of city planning is the art of creating outdoor spaces. These can be large or small, connected with walkways, avenues, alleys. A lot of the joy in the city comes from the changing rhythms of the spaces in it. City Building is essentially designing these spaces so they have harmony, surprise, energy, and peace; so that they link together in interesting ways.

The usefulness of buildings in our appreciation of a city is that they define for us the edges of public spaces. It does not much matter what goes on inside the buildings as far our as enjoyment of the city is concerned. Most of the buildings in a city could be totally filled with concrete without affecting our enjoyment of the city in the slightest. Even churches.

In Italy most of the city churches are not the free-standing structures we regard as traditional. In Rome almost all the churches are attached to other buildings. They are embedded in the urban fabric and serve to define urban space. We have, side-by-side, the butcher, the baker, the church, and the computer maker. Sometimes all we see of the church building is the doorway. This produces an intensely rich streetscape, and bears witness to the churches role in the immediacy of city life. Many examples are illustrated in "The Art of City Building",[9] an 1899 study by Camillo Sitte.

People have enjoyed cities for thousands of years but in 1889 Sitte was the first to bring this into consciousness by analyzing what creates our enjoyment. In doing this he discovered something that had always been known, that people enjoy the extraordinary richness that results from shaping and orchestrating the spaces they occupy. Previous to this, urban design had consisted of taking an existing city and inserting into it some public squares, axes, ceremonial routes and monuments, usually

---

8. Sitte, *Der Stadtbau*.

to glorify some temporary tyrant. People generally preferred to be in parts of the city that had not benefited from this design expertise. Baron Haussmann, as Prefect of the Seine, subjected Paris to this treatment in the 1860s. He opened up long vistas, allegedly so cannonballs could be shot down them to keep an unruly populace in order. He treated the streets of Paris as if it were a vast pinball machine, and introduced the word "Haussmannize" into the language, which means to widen and straighten streets as part of a rebuilding program. It has overtones of arrogance and insensitivity.

The same process took place in the United States after the war. Under the banner of Urban Renewal existing houses and stores were razed, communities were disrupted, the fabric of neighborhoods was destroyed, and huge new buildings were erected to house those that had been displaced. Unfortunately, not everyone appreciated the improvements that were offered by these planned communities. In the new impersonal neighborhoods only the gangs had a sense of belonging. The large buildings on vast open spaces that had appeared as part of the new order deteriorated rapidly. They became centers of alienation, crime, and despair.

The world's most notable urban failure is Brasilia, the new capital of Brazil, which was designed as a result of an architectural competition. The plan that seduced the jury by its elegant simplicity was based on a pair of crossed axes. These formed the framework on which everything was hung. The elegant simplicity of the plan made it impossible to achieve in reality the complex richness which people enjoy in a city. The sheer orderliness of the plan eliminated all anticipation, discovery, and surprise. Brasilia offers nothing to the pedestrian; it is boring, lonely, and unsafe. There are no urban precincts, no rich mix of experiences, very few places where people can gather. Only government workers live in the city in the equivalent of gated communities distributed on one of the axes of the cross. The other axis is reserved for a five kilometer spread of government and institutional buildings. The vast number of workers needed to service this community are obliged to live in a surrounding poverty belt of crowded favelas an hour's bus-ride away. There is no excuse for this: Brasilia was conceived fifty years after Sitte's book had been published. It survives only because it is a national capital and governments have the power to direct people to live there.

FIGURE 6. Space for enjoyment. The Cathedral Plaza in Salzburg as seen from the archway in the Residence Plaza. The Capital Plaza is beyond.

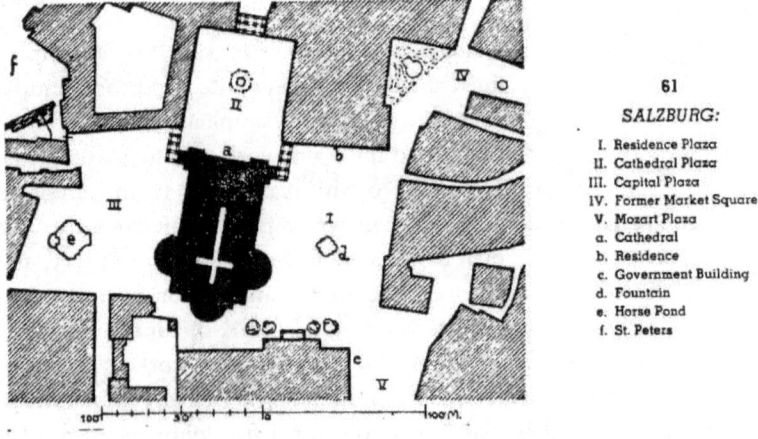

FIGURE 7. The City as Art. An alternating succession of spaces broad and narrow creates a rich and varied urban experience. The plan is from Camillo Sitte's "Der Stadtbau" of 1889.

What these vast failures have in common is that they ignore the importance of creating spaces that people will enjoy. Sitte's great contribution was to recognize the richness of urban environments that had accreted over the centuries and to formulate the principles by which new ones could be created. His methodology was to measure and draw plans of urban precincts, all to the same scale (just as the plans in this book are all drawn to the same scale of 1/1,000th of full size) so you can compare them. Sitte then equated the size, forms, and layout of the spaces he saw on the plans with the pleasure he found in being on the street. His plans do not differentiate the functions of the buildings he illustrates, except if the building is a church he puts a cross on it. The enjoyment of his spaces derives directly from the forms and connections of the spaces themselves and the human pursuits they foster. In studying his plans, one of which is illustrated in Figure 7, one notices that the white areas, representing space, are more interesting than the forms of the shaded areas which represent buildings, and although the spaces are irregular they have a kind of internal rhythm. Some of the public squares are connected to other squares by their corners, so in leaving an open space we pass into a very tight and constricted passageway before bursting forth into another open space. This is illustrated by a present-day photograph of the central area of Salzburg (figure 6) which is taken from the Residence Plaza looking through the arcade to the Cathedral Plaza. The function of many of the buildings may have changed since Sitte's time, but the spatial layout and the interest it generates have endured. Notice how the entrances to the squares are offset from the exits, so we do not see the endless continuous vistas beloved by Baron Haussmann. Imagine what it must feel like to be forced to walk close to the towering wall of the cathedral in passing from one square to another; we not only see the cathedral from across the square, we are also forced to confront it close-up, to experience the texture of its stonework and the chill of its shadow.

In 1970 I used these principles to design the public spaces surrounding the Church of the Holy Trinity in Toronto, illustrated in figure 96, page 178. This historic church found itself in the middle of a major urban redevelopment and by virtue of its position it was able to influence the form of that development. By a complicated three-way system of land exchanges between the church, the developer, and the City of Toronto, streets were closed and lot lines were redrawn so in exchange for the old churchyard a linkage of pedestrian spaces was created around the church. Two old houses owned by the church were moved out of the path of urban renewal: they were jacked up off their foundations and pirouetted to their new locations closer to the church. Here they define a small urban square in the manner beloved by Camillo Sitte, creating an oasis of peace in the center of the city. The white areas of Sitte's plans are for street markets, parks, revolutionary posters, conversations, sidewalk cafés, parking lots, fountains, pigeons, bicycles, parades, street musicians, window shopping, parades, newspapers, families, and walking the dog. Space is wonderful, rich with potential.

Typographers are aware of the importance of space. They have a word—the counter—for the white space contained in a letter. Thus a capital O in Adobe Minion Pro (the typeface used for this book) was designed not as a ring of black ink but as an exquisitely-shaped white space bounded by an undulating wall of varying thickness. This serves to distinguish an elegantly crafted inner space from the rest of our space which is full of stuff: oxygen and armchairs, temples and teapots. George Spencer-Brown opens his *Laws of Form*[10] with the words "Let there be a distinction." This is more an invitation than a dogmatic declaration. It offers a choice. A small room might be considered intimate if it were bounded by walls and the window was tiny. The walls would serve as a distinction between inner space and the rest of outer space. However if the same room were part of a condo development where the windows consisted of floor-to-ceiling glass such a room could be considered expansive. Our concept of this space would depend on what we would choose to regard as its boundaries: its walls or the distant horizon. However, a blind person would continue to regard such a room, even with glass all round, as intimate. So our concept of a space is conditional on our interpretation of the clues it presents to us.

**Creative Space**

A unique aspect of space is its creative power. In fact recent discoveries indicate that it is the creative potential of space that could have created the entire universe. A problem that had been troubling mathematicians and cosmologists for a long time is that the universe contains lots of stuff, sometimes in massive amounts, but where did all this mass come from? When a new particle is created it travels at the speed of light, and the Theory of Relativity holds that to attain that speed

---

9. Spencer-Brown, *Laws of Form*, 1.

its mass would have to be zero. So what sort of creative process created the mass we see all around us? Where did all this mass come from? In 1964 Peter Higgs and five others discovered in a mathematical relationship a possibility that would permit the existence of a particle whose speed would be less that the speed of light, and its reduced speed would allow it to have a positive mass. This theoretical particle was named the Higgs boson after Peter Higgs. At that time the only evidence for it was a single page of mathematical equations indicating a theoretical possibility.

According to quantum-field theory every field has an associated quantum particle, so if the Higgs boson exists there would have to be a Higgs field with which the Higgs boson is associated. This field would be an energy field that exists everywhere and fills all space. The field uses its particle, the Higgs boson, to interact continuously with other particles. As particles pass through the field they acquire energy from the field. This energy creates a relative mass, so a particle that was formerly without mass slows down because it has become "heavier". The Higgs field, if it exists, could be the mechanism by which particles acquire the mass necessary for them to be able to attract one another, and without such mass they would float around freely as individual particles at the speed of light, and not be able to combine together to form either matter or us.

The possibility that the Higgs field could be the agency for creating matter from empty space captured the imagination of scientists everywhere. It would not be possible to verify the existence of the Higgs field directly, but if its associated particle, the Higgs boson, could be detected that would provide evidence of the existence of the Higgs field. The boson, too, could not be detected directly, but its presence could be deduced from its interaction with other particles. To force this interaction a vast accelerator, the Large Hadron Collider, was built by the European Organization for Nuclear Research (CERN) with headquarters in Geneva. It consisted of a circular tunnel with a circumference of 27 kilometers buried 100 meters underground and traversing the French/Swiss border. Here collisions between opposing beams of protons reproduce the conditions that existed within a billionth of a second after the Big Bang, 14 billion years ago. On the 14th of March 2013 the Collider confirmed that among the traces of particles scattered by collision a particle had been detected with the fundamental criteria for a Higgs boson. The detection of the Higgs boson confirmed the existence of the Higgs field, an agency by which space is able to create matter.

**Visions of Space**

How do we perceive space? We cannot see it. Where there is most space there is the least to see. The light from the sun come to us through ninety-three million miles of space, and even more kilometers. That's a lot of space. So because light passes through space unimpeded, space cannot be seen. All we can see are objects on the other side of space. How

FIGURE 8. Flying high in Grand Central Terminal.

then do we perceive space? We can derive some clues from the way we describe space. Take for example a very high space such as the main hall at New York's famed Grand Central Terminal (figure 8). We would describe this space as soaring, uplifting, releasing.

FIGURE 9. Overburden at Lourdes, the Basilica Pius X.

Take a very low space (figure 9) such as the Basilica Pius X, the underground shrine at Lourdes in France. We would describe this space as crushing, oppressing.

FIGURE 10. A stretch in the London Underground, the pedestrian walkway at the South Kensington station.

Take a very long space (figure 10) such as the passageway at the South Kensington Station on the London Underground. We would describe that space as stretching, extending. What all these descriptions have in common is that they are all verbs, they all relate to things we can do with our bodies. We can leap and soar and crush and stretch. These are all human capabilities. Of course we are not really stretched and crushed. No matter how I stretched I could not reach the twenty foot high ceiling at Lourdes. The structure was designed by Dr. Freyssinet, a renowned engineer who was one of my professors so I am sure I am in no danger of being crushed; but at the same time I feel that crushing weight overhead, and in Grand Central Terminal I walk on the floor like everybody else, while feeling like flying.

Space is described in terms of our bodies. We imagine what we would have to do in order to experience what we perceive as the quality of that space, and then we describe the space as if it were itself performing these actions. We describe space by identifying with it, and then looking inside ourselves. Some people with acrophobia, a fear of heights, can become terrified when looking up at a tall building even though they are standing safely on the sidewalk. That is because they experience the height of a building in terms of their body falling off the top of it and hurtling downwards. This is a gripping way to experience the space demarcated by a tall building.

Excitement apart, is it not wonderful that space, the most immaterial quantity we can imagine, is experienced by our bodies, our closest contact with the material world. Space can dance and sing, space can laugh, space can wonder, space can worship, space speaks to us. And if it can speak to us space must have meaning. The joy of architecture, going beyond mere building, is its expression of space.

When we perceive space in this way, with our bodies, we are not consciously looking at it. Certainly we use our eyes when perceiving space, but not in the same way as we do when we are looking at an object. When we look at an object we focus our eyes on it and subject every part of it to scrutiny. It is as if we were checking-off all the details of an object against a check-list in order to "recognize" it. This process requires effort. It is as if we were projecting our consciousness out of ourselves into the material world, and this can be tiring. Museum directors, custodians of vast collections of objects, know all about this: how we can become exhausted after just a couple of hours of looking. That is why the museum cafeteria is so popular.

The process of perceiving space operates on a different basis. Instead of projecting our consciousness outside ourselves we relax and let awareness enter ourselves, which it does instantly. We do not stare at anything in particular. We just hold ourselves open to what is around us. In fact I have discovered that the best way to experience the space in a church is to visit it at night and sit in the dark. Usually the light that filters in from stars and streetlights will be enough to perceive the general forms of the space but not the distractions. The furnishings, signs, colors, details and decoration will all be suppressed. If the space is internal, or if it is really dark, a single candle will be enough to illuminate it. I have learned more about a space by spending half an hour sitting in a pew in the dark than by spending a whole day in measuring, sketching, recording, and studying. The only difficulty I have found is in convincing the Sexton that sitting in the dark is not some weird mystical rite (but perhaps it is!). All custodians seem to want to show off the full power of their lighting systems, flipping switches until the shrine looks like a supermarket. It is not always easy to persuade them of the value of those perceptions that are received from the silence and the dark.

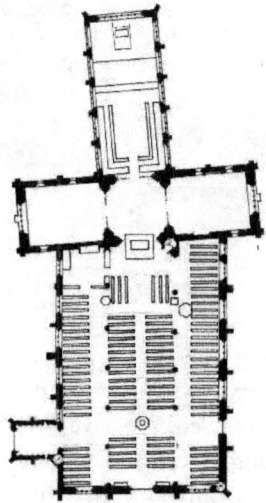

FIGURE 11. The Church of the Holy Trinity, Stratford-upon-Avon, showing how the "weeping chancel" is tilted to the left.

## Interpretations of Space

From earliest times the church has been known as the Body of Christ. This term was applied to the altar, to the gathering of worshipers,

FIGURE 12. Interior of The Church of the Holy Trinity, Stratford-upon-Avon. Note that in the photograph the east window is off-center in the chancel arch.

and to the church building itself. This was not a metaphor, a poetic form of expression; it was a precise description of the way that the community and the building were perceived. We have already seen how we perceive the space within a building in terms of our bodies—the space in Christ's building was perceived as Christ's body. The space of the chancel was identified with the head, the nave with the body, the transepts with the outstretched arms, and most importantly the crossing with the heart. Tradition has it that when Our Lord suffered death on the cross his head fell to the left, so in some medieval churches the chancel was also turned slightly to the left, creating a so-called "weeping chancel". When in such a church a natural response is for us to turn our heads slightly to the left; a gentle offering of ourselves to express a unity with the Savior.

# The Meaning of Space

An example is The Church of the Holy Trinity in Stratford-upon-Avon (figure 11) where the plan clearly shows how the chancel is inclined, although it is hard to make this out on the postcards sold in the church gift shop. The photographer, considering the angularity to be an error, stationed himself on the bisector of the two axes, hoping to minimize the effect of this deviance. Perhaps he could have corrected this ancient error in PhotoShop.

**Holy Ground**

All nations, all cultures, embrace the concept of holy places, holy ground. This is a natural attribute of all people, part of our humanity. Some people might try to deny it or wish that it were not so, but it is hard to deny a concept that is so universal. We all know of religions that are big on shrines—there we would expect to find reverence for sacred space. However in order to show that sacred space is a universal concept we would have to encounter it also in those religions that exist mainly in the mind or in the spirit, in those communities that pride themselves on not being into real estate.

Unity Church, with a headquarters at Unity Village in Missouri, has a prayer ministry. Every day hundreds of requests are phoned in at 1-800-NOW-PRAY (1-800-669-7729). Every month over two million meditation booklets are mailed all over the world. This is a church that ministers by mail and phone. It must be the most transcendent of ministries, and yet included in their message is an honoring of sacred space. One of the ministers of the Unity Church, in describing how a counseling meeting was influenced by its surroundings[11] says: "We sat together in the front row. The little room was quiet, and the loving consciousness of the people who had been there for services the day before still lingered in the quiet of its walls." . . . a beautiful evocation of a sacred space.

The Society of Friends, a down-to-earth denomination whose liturgy would seem to be the least likely to embrace the concept of sacred space, published in its Journal[12]:"Places and things do not hallow people,

---

10. Pierson, *Daily Word*.

11. Nicholson, *A Hallowed Place*.

but the enduring faith of the people may hallow places where there has been unbroken prayer and worship, generation after generation."

Much of the worship of the Salvation Army takes place in the street, without any buildings, yet in their worship is an acknowledgement of sacred space. In Canada their outdoor summer meetings at Jackson's Point thrill to Major Ryan's chorus "Holy Ground"[13] based on Exodus 3:5: "Take off your shoes, for this is holy ground!"

FIGURE 13. The small stepped-pyramid structure built into the wall of the Kremlin houses the mortal remains of Comrade Lenin. In Red Square pilgrims stand in line.

Even a nation founded on the principles of atheism welcomes pilgrims to Lenin's Tomb. Red Square (figure 13) has taken on the attributes of sacred space. This did not happen by accident. Stalin, in his youth, was educated at a seminary in Tiflis, and he was familiar with the power of religious ritual. He was also familiar with Karl Marx's famous aphorism "religion is the opiate of the people." In fact, he wanted a people that would be passive and manageable, so Lenin's tomb of glass was set in a

---

12. Ryan, *A New Holiness Chorus*.

building in the form of a stepped pyramid, which is a form associated with many ancient religions. This had two functions—it presented the remains of Lenin as an object of veneration for the people, and at the same time it demonstrated that Comrade Lenin was thoroughly dead. Stalin wanted to have a religious figurehead associated with the state to strengthen his own grip on it, but he did not want to create a Messiah. He did not want to offer any encouragement to a political movement based on a resurrected Lenin that could threaten his rule—an earlier version of "Elvis Lives!"

**Architecture for Worship**

Some people are made profoundly uncomfortable by the concept of sacred space, with its associations of myth and magic. It brings us uncomfortably close to confronting a part of our nature that is dark, irrational, unpredictable, and unsafe. The liturgical logician asks "If God is an all-pervading spirit, if God is everywhere, why do we need a special place to worship Him?" The argument is logical but people are not that logical, and perhaps God is not that spiritual. We worship in special places, in special rituals, not because God is more there than anywhere else but because that is where it is easiest for us to perceive God. Sacred space is where we have an enhanced awareness of the holy presence. It releases the worshiper, it does not confine the worshiped. In sundry places the Bible demands that we "remember the Sabbath and keep it holy"[14]. In the space-time continuum this means setting aside special times and special spaces for worship: it means making a sacrifice in our lives and in our world.

"Architecture for Worship" is the title of a book by Edward Sovik which I revere for its content and reject for its argument, like a wise teacher from whom one has learned much and with whom one disagrees. Sovik is an architect and a philosopher with a clear rational approach to architecture for worship. Luckily for us his architecture is not as rational as his philosophy. He reasons that: "... because God is everywhere there can be no holy places in the world, not even the stable at Bethlehem nor the upper room in Jerusalem." As a philosopher he denies that we have a need for what he calls "cultic spaces" which we achieve by "isolating

---

13. Exod. 20:8, 31:14; Lev. 25:1-8; Deut. 5:12

places and ascribing to the place a particular holiness", and then, as an architect, he tells us how to design such spaces. He writes[15]:

> "The space which is ultimately faithful to the Christian vision will be one in which the room is devoid of any explicitly cultic images or furnishings... The church's architecture ought to be absolutely forthright, entirely authentic, without deceits or illusions, without artificialities of any sort. Anyone who thinks this kind of authenticity comes easily, or even cheaply, is mistaken. Our civilization is so abundantly supplied with substitutes, artifices, artificialities and the ersatz that the search for the genuine thing is sometimes long and expensive."

FIGURE 14. A gymnasium for a rigorous workout of the faith. Trinity United Methodist Church in Charles City, Iowa, takes the ordinary to fresh heights of accomplishment. The architect is E.A. Sovik.

The question that is begged here is: Why pursue the genuine? If God is everywhere God is also in the trashy, the ugly, and the fake. If we can worship equally well anywhere, why even write a book on Architecture for Worship? Luckily Sovik did not pursue this argument and as a result

---

14. Sovik, *Architecture for Worship*, 56.

# The Meaning of Space

FIGURE 16. The aesthetics of the ordinary extend into the central courtyard of Trinity United Methodist Church. Notice the shadows of the bells on the garden wall.

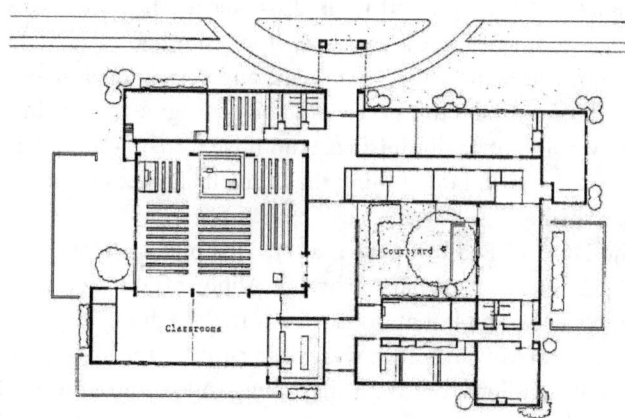

FIGURE 15. Plan of Trinity United Methodist Church. Sliding screens enable the worship area to expand into the adjacent classrooms.

we have his book and his work. Sovik's life's work has been to create special spaces for worship, and to do this in the manner of the ordinary. Like the Shakers he raises the ordinary to exquisite heights of accomplishment. He creates very beautiful sacred spaces (see figs. 14, 15, 16) in a style that could be called Neo-Secular. He creates a rational, clear, and orderly architecture in order to induce in the congregation a worshipful state of mind, a purpose he shares with flagellant brotherhoods, holy rollers, and feather-decked shamans smoking strange tobaccos. What is interesting is that even those who dismiss the concept of sacred space may end up in the company of those creating it.

**Space for Worship**

Sacred space is not space where God is, for God is everywhere. Evelyn Underhill writes[16]: "There must be a sense in which the whole world and everything in it is sacred to us because God loves it." However there are some places where it is easier for us to be aware of God's love, and these places are called sacred spaces. It is not as if there were a limited quantity of holiness to go around, and in blessing one spot we deprive the rest. Sacred space relates not to the presence of God but to the perception of the people.

At first one might think that the holiness of holy ground has been impregnated into the ground itself. This is a result of our old habit of thinking in terms of what is material. If we could go to some holy site, engage some earth-moving equipment, and scrape off a few hundred cubic yards of topsoil, I think we would have to agree that the holiness of the place would not be diminished. And if we were to dump that topsoil in front of City Hall, I don't think the municipal offices would suddenly become a shrine.

The Duke of Bedford gave it a try. He bought a Holy Well which had been built in Leigh Barton by the Abbot of Tavistock. He had it dismantled and re-built it at his estates at Endsleigh in Devon. However there is no record of anybody having been cured of the dropsy by visiting the well at its new location. With charming candor one of the neighbors[17] said: "We thought it a most strange thing that the Bedford's had moved the well to Endsleigh. After all, the water in it can hardly be holy now that they've moved it from the original spring."

So the holiness of holy ground obtains not from holy material but from the holy space it occupies. It is non-transferable. Space is made sacred by the clear intention and purposeful dedication of those who

---

15. Underhill: *Mixed Pasture*
16. Foot: *Following the Tamar.*

create it. Space is made sacred by a holy act; by sacraments, prayer and healing. It is where the miracle of the incarnation has taken place. Sacred space is created in the inner silence of a sacred act. It offers the Pause That Refreshes.

> *In sacred space our bodies and Christ's Body can co-exist.*
> *He in us, and we in Him.*

**Summary of Chapter 2: The Meaning of Space**

1. Space, often regarded as a negative, is important because it is always capable of being filled by a variety of solid things.

2. Space is a potential for action.
Space is nothing, waiting for something.
Space is what was and is not, or what is yet to be.
Space is feminine.
Space is creative.
Space is freedom.

3 Urban design is the art of creating outdoor spaces that will have individual characters, and offer us a variety of experiences while serving a variety of functions.

4. We describe space in terms of our bodies. We imagine what we would have to do in order to experience the quality of the space, and then we describe the space as if it were itself performing these actions: space may be considered as a verb.

5. Thus space is expressive; it is able to elicit an emotion or convey a meaning.

6. Sacred space may convey a sacred meaning. Space has a potential to worship, and by this it is able to assist us in our worship.

# Chapter 3
# The Anatomy of Worship

In the last chapter we learned that there are six ways by which space can support worship. In this chapter we will learn that Christian worship also can be expressed in exactly six ministries, and each of these ministries can be related to one of Rudolf Schwarz's Six Plans. However we know that scripture demands that all churches must embrace all six ministries, so a diagram of pathways is offered to show ways in which compatible ministries may be connected. Let's explore . . .

The word "Worship" derives from the Old English *woerthscipe* (worth-ship) *woerth* = value, *scipe* = condition Worship is the expression and celebration of a revered relationship of praise and thanksgiving; a relationship between

> the People.
>
> the Sacraments, and
>
> the World.

These are the three parameters[18], or defining terms or entities, in Christian worship. I'll call them parameters.

The People are those gathered to hear and proclaim the Word, and to share in Holy Communion.

What is a Sacrament? Those of us who had to learn their catechism from the old Book of Common Prayer will remember a sacrament as being "an outward and visible sign of an inner and spiritual grace" The Sacraments of Baptism and Holy Communion and the readings of scripture are channels by which God's grace is imparted to us.

The World is the totality of God's creation, the context of our humanity.

Worship is about relationship. This term, relationship, also occurs in mathematics. If we apply the mathematics of permutations to the three

---

17. A parameter is a factor whose value determines the form or character of an operation.

# The Anatomy of Worship

parameters of worship we find that there are six, and only six, possible relationships between them. That is: these three parameters, taken two-at-a-time, may be combined into exactly six permutations, each of which expresses a unique relationship. From this we can deduce that there are six ways in which worship can express itself. The mathematical underpinning for the six expressions of worship can be demonstrated by creating a tree, rather like a family tree

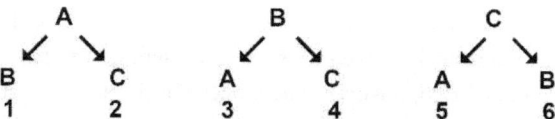

FIGURE 17. A tree, showing there are six possible relationships[19] between pairs of three parameters, here indicated by the letters A, B, and C.

An early example showing how six relationships may be generated by pairing three parameters is found in the Kabbalah, an ancient system of Jewish theosophy, theurgy, and mysticism developed by rabbis from the seventh century in which is found the phrase "Three s₀nes make six houses". A translation of the whole passage occurs in Umberto Eco's novel "Foucault's Pendulum"[20]. It reads: "Two stones make two houses. Three stones make six houses. Four stones make twenty-four houses. Five stones make one hundred and twenty houses. Six stones make seven hundred and twenty houses. Seven stones make five thousand and forty houses. Beyond this point, think of what the mouth cannot say and the ear cannot hear."

18. This can also be deduced by substituting in the general formula

$$P_{n,r} = \frac{n!}{(n-r)!}$$

where P is the number of possible relationships, n is the number of parameters, r is the size of the group, and "!" indicates factorial. Thus substituting for 3 parameters grouped in 2's:

$$P_{3,2} = \frac{3 \times 2 \times 1}{(3-2)} = 6$$

19. Eco, Foucault's Pendulum.

Relationship is a vector, which means: it has a direction. The relationship of A-to-B is not the same as the relationship of B-to-A. As an example, my relationship to you, dear Reader, is quite different from your relationship to me. My relationship to you consists of my making a unique Body of Knowledge available to you for your information, instruction, and delight. Crudely put, your relationship to me involves your paying a considerable amount of cash to my publishers in the hope that some of it will trickle down to me.

The mathematical computation is valuable because by establishing that pairs of the three parameters of worship may be combined in six, and only six, relationships we know we have defined the field. We have established that Christian worship may occur in six, and only six, distinct ministries, and these embrace all the possibilities for worship. Knowing this, we don't have to cast about looking for a seventh ministry. Anything that looks like a seventh ministry will turn out to be a thinly-disguised version of one of the other six.

What are these ministries? By considering the qualities of each relationship between parameters we can deduce which ministry it represents. The six ministries are set out in order of the presence and focus of the worshipers, ranging from the introspective ministry of Contemplation to the extremely extroverted ministry of Justice.

**The Six Ministries**

Here are set out the six ministries formed by the pairing of parameters:

1. For the first ministry, the relationship is: People-to-Sacrament. The People approach the Sacrament with awe, to adore and meditate on the divine presence. This is the ministry of Contemplation.

2. For the second ministry, Sacred Meeting, the relationship is: Sacrament-to-People. The Sacrament is brought to the People to heal, forgive, reconcile and bless. This is the ministry of Pastoral Care.

3. For the third ministry, the relationship is: Sacrament-to-World. The light of the Sacrament shines out into the World, to proclaim Christ's presence. This is the ministry of Witness.

4. For the fourth ministry the relationship is: World-to-People. The World becomes a path for the People, who band themselves together for a common purpose. This is the ministry of Dedication.

5. For the fifth ministry the relationship is: World-to-Sacrament. The World is invited to approach and share the Sacrament and share in communion with Christ. This is the ministry of Evangelism.

6. For the sixth ministry the relationship is: People-to-World. The People go out into the World to secure justice, peace, freedom, and fulfillment for all. This is the ministry of Justice.

I cannot over-emphasize the importance of keeping in mind these three parameters. They create the six ministries of Christian worship. Without them we could have fifty ministries to deal with, and still not be sure that our list was complete. It is the invocation of these parameters, creating six ministries, that enables us to link space and worship so we can truly serve our congregations.

In the sixth ministry, when the people have gone out into the world they have departed from the sacraments, they have left their safe haven and are exposed to danger. They have to carry within themselves the security of the faith. Inwardly the People have to embody the Sacrament, which is the relationship of the first ministry: the ministry of Contemplation.

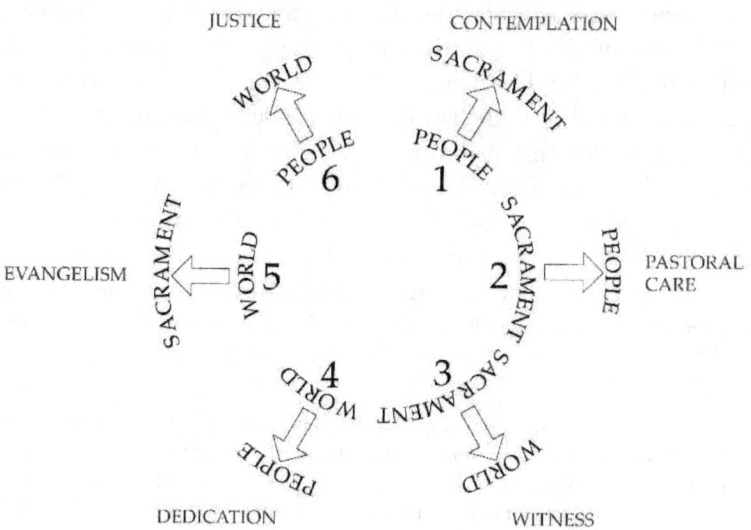

FIGURE 18. The Cycle of Worship, showing the six possible relationships of its three constituent parameters. These relationships between pairs of parameters are numbered on the inner ring, and outboard of them are names for the six ministries they generate.

Thus the sixth ministry fosters the first ministry creating a ring (figure 18). All the names given to the ministries are approximations. Their true meaning should be deduced from the relationship of the parameters. For example, the ministry of Contemplation could as well be called meditation or adoration.

> Pastoral Care includes healing and reconciliation,
>
> Witness includes proclamation and preaching,
>
> Dedication includes vocation and stewardship
>
> Evangelism includes invitation, sharing and radical welcome
>
> Justice includes liberation, peace and the environment.

Other ministries can be placed in their correct category not by attempting to match titles but by discovering which relationship of parameters best describes its process.

**Discovering a New Foundation**

I remember, years ago, when I was reading Simone Weil's[21] "*Waiting on God*"[22], how surprised I was when her phrase ". . . the six petitions of the Our Father . . . " suddenly jumped off the page at me. Immediately, I checked the wording of the Lord's Prayer. I found it did indeed contain six petitions. Not only that; the six petitions had the same order and purpose as the six ministries I had listed in the Cycle of Worship! To this day I remember my sense of awe at that revelation—the world was suddenly a different place. It demanded a change of focus, a change of career. It demanded that I give up my architectural partnership to pursue this knowledge wherever it should lead. Since then I have had to focus

---

20. Simone Weil, 1909–1943, a French philosopher and theologian, had a life troubled by ill-health and conflict. As a communist sympathizer she worked for a year in the Renault Works to experience solidarity with the workers; and she traveled to Barcelona to oppose Franco's fascist rule. Originally an atheist, she embraced the Catholic faith but considered herself unworthy for baptism, so although she attended mass every day she never received the sacrament. Her elder brother, André Weil, a mathematician, was noted for his contributions to number theory, which perhaps explains her interest in the numbers associated with prayer. All her works were published posthumously.

21. Weil, *Waiting on God*, 153.

my life on promoting this knowledge, on lecturing, teaching, writing, and consulting with churches who wish to renew their worship space.

The six petitions in the Lord's Prayer follow the same sequence of relationships between People, Sacrament and World as is depicted in the Cycle of Worship (figure 27). These six ministries are Contemplation, Pastoral Care, Witness, Dedication, Evangelism, and Justice. They correspond to the six petitions that are included in the Lord's Prayer. Their order also corresponds to the order of the Six Plans of Rudolf Schwarz.

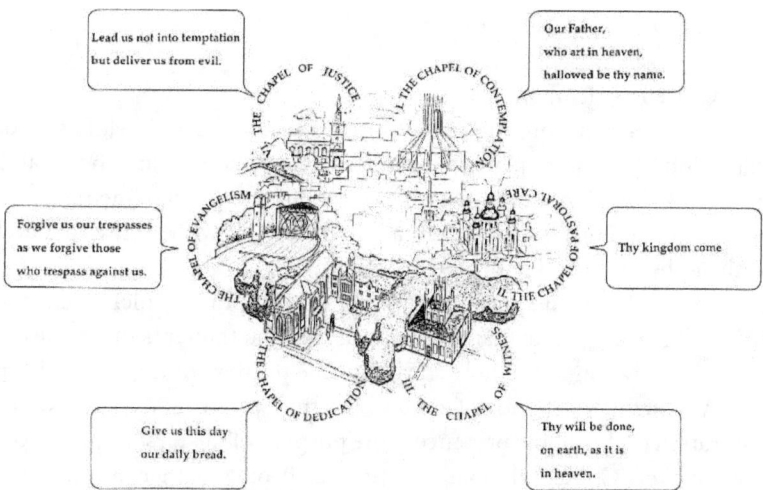

I. The Metropolitan Cathedral of Christ the King, Liverpool.

II. Holy Trinity Ukrainian Orthodox Cathedral, Winnipeg.

III Temple of the Children of Peace, Sharon, Ontario.

IV Trinity College Chapel, University of Toronto.

V Heilig Kreuz Kirche, Bottrop, Germany.

VI St. James Church Piccadilly, London.

FIGURE 19. The Cycle of Six Chapels praying the six petitions in the Our Father. The six ministries are also related to the Six Plans. This is the litany recited by the six chapels:

I have made an illustration (figure 19) to show how each of the six ministries of the Christian church is linked both to a petition in the Our Father and to one of Schwarz's Six Plans. Each Plan is indicated by a sketch of an actual example of a church built from such a plan, each one taken from a chapter in a following section which is titled "Churches Built with the Six Plans". The cycle of six ministries therefore may be regarded as a choir of six chapels, each endlessly leading us in the six petitions of the prayer our Savior taught us. Simone Weil writes: "This prayer is so simple, so perfect, it embraces all our duties and desires . . . we cannot conceive of any prayer that is not already contained in it—it is to prayer what Christ is to humanity"

1. Hallowed be thy name.

The first petition, the prayer offered in the first chapel, is one of adoration. We contemplate the wonder of God's holy Name: the great "I am". This duty is demanded of us by the First Commandment: "Thou shalt love the Lord thy God with all thy heart and with all thy soul and with all thy mind and with all thy strength" (Exod. 20:3-1)

Adoration is the purpose of the prayer for purity which opens the Mass. This prayer asks that God will cleanse the thoughts of our hearts by the inspiration of the holy spirit, but the purpose of this purification is so we may perfectly love God and worthily praise God's holy Name. Adoration of the divine presence is the purpose of the First Ministry, the ministry of Contemplation, where the People gather around the Sacrament.

2. Thy kingdom come

The coming of God's kingdom will comfort all sorrow, satisfy all hunger, heal all wounds, forgive all sins. All souls will be made whole by the Holy Spirit. This is the fulfillment of the ministry of Pastoral Care, which includes healing, and reconciliation. This is the charge of the Second Ministry. The coming of the Kingdom is represented in the Cycle of Worship, (figure 18, page 35), by the Sacrament spreading its blessings over God's People.

3. Thy will be done on earth, as it is in heaven.

The ministry of Witness proclaims that God is with us, that God's presence permeates the world, even though heaven is not yet achieved on earth. By holding on to a vision of heaven as a model for earth, by seeing the Christ in ourselves and one another, by caring for our planet, we are able in a small way to be witnesses to the fulfilling of God's will in the world. This is represented in the Cycle of Worship by the Sacrament sending its influence out over the World.

4. Give us this day our daily bread.

Our daily bread springs from the work of many hands: hands sowing, reaping, threshing, milling, baking, buying, selling. The bread on our table represents also the work of our own hands: we have purchased it with part of what we have earned from our labors. So this petition honors our work and the work of all people. It is a prayer that in the world we will have work which we can dedicate to God and to the support of our neighbors and ourselves. It is also a prayer for the feeding of those in the world who have no work. The bread is what we need for our daily sustenance. Our dedication is a daily dedication which we will repeat tomorrow and for all our tomorrows, a dedication to our vocation and our daily duty. The World is the workplace for the laborers in the fields of the Lord, it is the path for the People on their journey through life.

5. Forgive us our trespasses as we forgive those that trespass against us.

To forgive those that trespass against us we have to go out into the world and restore our relationships. We have to do this before we ourselves can be forgiven. We have to be reconciled to the World before we can share in the Sacraments. This reflects the fifth relationship in the Cycle of Worship, a relationship that reflects a movement from World to Sacrament, a movement that carries the world along with it. This reconciliation to one another is demanded of us by Christ's words: "If you are offering your gift at the altar, and there remember your brother has something against you, leave your gift at the altar and go; first be reconciled to your brother, and then come and offer your gift." (Mathew 5:23)

This is a uniquely Christian concept, not found in previous Jewish usage[23]. It sets a new direction for Christ's church. It's not enough for us to say "I forgive you", perhaps feeling very noble when we do so. We can

---

22. Charles, Religious Development, Ch. 5.

only be forgiven when our neighbors are reconciled to us. We have to leave our church and go out into the world to forgive our brothers and sisters, and to have them forgive us. We have to re-create and make whole our relationship with them. Only then can we re-enter the church and ourselves be forgiven. This ministry then involves much coming and going—going out into the world and inviting others to return with us to share in the sacrament. This shows Evangelism to be a warmly personal ministry of sharing. In the Cycle of Worship the fifth ministry shows the whole World being brought to the Sacrament.

6. Lead us not into temptation, but deliver us from evil.

There is still much evil, injustice, and enslavement in the world. To redress this, to promote justice, is the charge of the sixth ministry. This does not mean that we must fight injustice—to do that would just replace one hostility by another. We must avoid becoming belligerent in our quest for peace. To quote from The Letter of James, 3:18: "True justice is the harvest reaped by peacemakers from seeds sown in a spirit of peace." We must avoid becoming rigid in our pursuit of freedom. We ask not to be led into these temptations. To allow the qualities of justice, peace, and harmony to manifest themselves in the outer world we have to first foster them within ourselves. We have to create in the inner what we seek to create in the outer. A whole People go out into a divided World, joyfully fulfilling the mission of the sixth ministry.

I wish I could claim that I had built up the ring of Six Plans on the foundation of the Our Father, but in fact it was not so. This structure was something I discovered, not something I created. My role was that of archeologist rather than that of architect, and in an archeological excavation the foundation is the last thing to be revealed.

**Expanding Worship**

To build a church for any particular form of worship, we now know how it should be planned. However in the real world churches are not built for just one aspect of worship: all churches have to be able to contain all six forms of worship. They may emphasize one form over another, but they should not totally exclude any. Just as the Order of Service may contain all the components of prayer, and the Our Father contains petitions for all the ministries; all church buildings need to shelter all the forms of worship.

A way to expand the ministry of the church—to make sure this happens—would be for a congregation to adopt a couple of "secondary ministries" to round out their repertoire. These are not of such importance as the primary ministry, but they do offer support for the primary ministry. They extend the use of space, and expand ministry. Thus the congregation would have a primary ministry reflecting its purpose, and two secondary ministries to extend its reach. The remaining three ministries it can accommodate from time to time, with a certain amount of improvisation.

**THE PRIMARY MINISTRY**

**2 SECONDARY MINISTRIES**

**3 OCCASIONAL MINISTRIES**

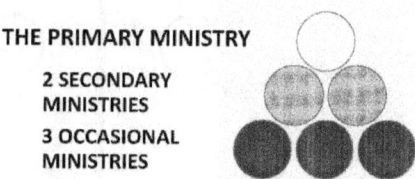

FIGURE 20. Expanding the role of the congregation's: choices of ministry.

We can't leave it up to the congregation to choose their secondary ministries because they would pick the ministries they felt most comfortable with. They would choose the ministries most similar to their Primary Ministry so they could avoid the discomfort of change. The ministries they would reject are precisely the ministries they would need to undertake if they wished to expand the range of their worship, so we can use the structure of the Ring of Worship to provide a way of identifying secondary ministries that will widen the scope of the congregations worship. The Cycle of Worship shows all the relationships between ministries, so within its structure it will also show us ways to combine them. An obvious choice for a secondary ministry would be that ministry which occurs on the opposite side of the ring to the primary ministry—its position almost implies opposite qualities.

## Opposite Ministries

Simone Weil[24] observed that of the six petitions in the Our Father, the first three petitions are transcendent and the last three are immanent; that is, in the first three petitions we praise and worship the universal Creator and in the last three we pray for our creaturely needs. The first three petitions contain the word "Thy"—Thy Name, Thy Kingdom, Thy Will . . . and the last three contain the word "Us"—feed us, forgive us, and

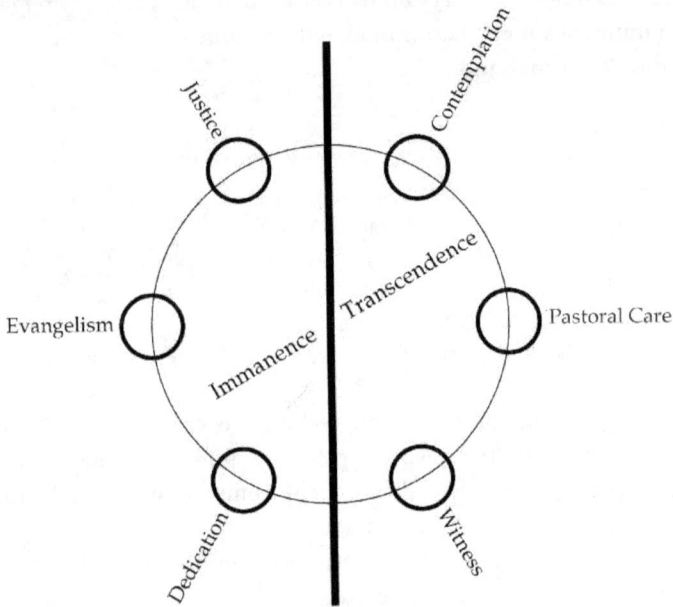

FIGURE 21. A vertical division of the Cycle of Ministry separates the qualities of Immanence and Transcendence.

lead us. If we set out the six petitions in an array, as in the Choir of Six Chapels (figure 19 on page 37) the qualities of transcendence, God in spirit, occur on the right side of the diagram and the qualities of immanence, God in the world, occur on the left. These qualities are carried through into worship, so if we draw a vertical line through the

23. Weil, Waiting on God, 153.

# The Anatomy of Worship

center of the Cycle of Worship (figure 21) we see that when a congregation adopts a secondary ministry on the opposite side of the Ring we cross the divide between immanence and transcendence, ensuring that the congregation will extend its reach by honoring both immanence and transcendence in its worship.

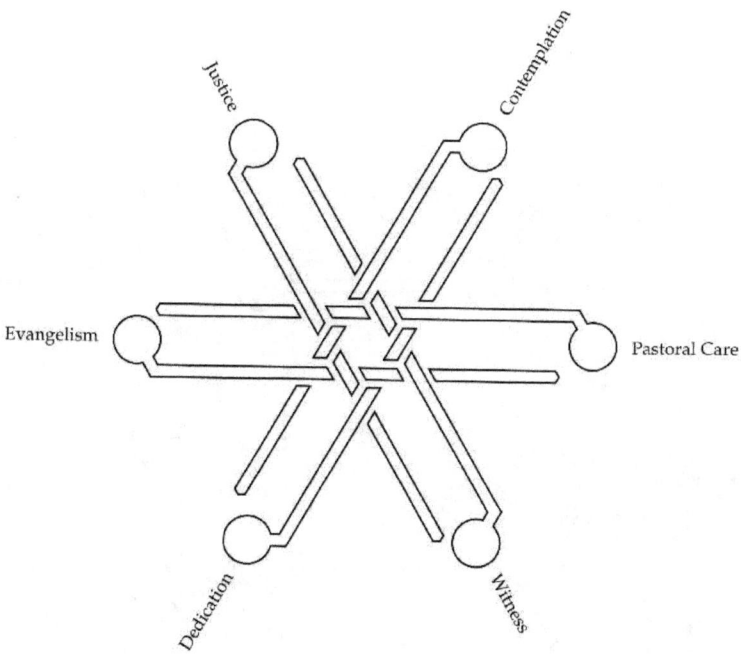

FIGURE 22. Opposite Ministries. Adopting ministries which occur diametrically opposite one another will ensure that a congregation's worship will be both immanent and transcendent.

A congregation that accepts such a pairing of ministries is enriched by undertaking to work both in the heart and in the world.

**Adjacent Ministries**

To round-out the role of the congregation by choosing an additional secondary ministry we could select a ministry which is adjacent to the primary one, but each ministry has two ministries next to it on the ring, one on each side, so which one should we choose? When we study the Cycle of Worship (figure 18, page 35), the diagram that sets out the six basic relationships of worship, we see that on the inner ring the parameters are paired: People comes next to People, Sacrament to Sacrament, and World to World. This means that these ministries in may be paired because although they share the same "subject" on the inner ring they have different "objects" on the outer ring, indicating a divergence of direction, just as the same congregation may, at different times, have a different focus. The ministries that are paired in this way are:

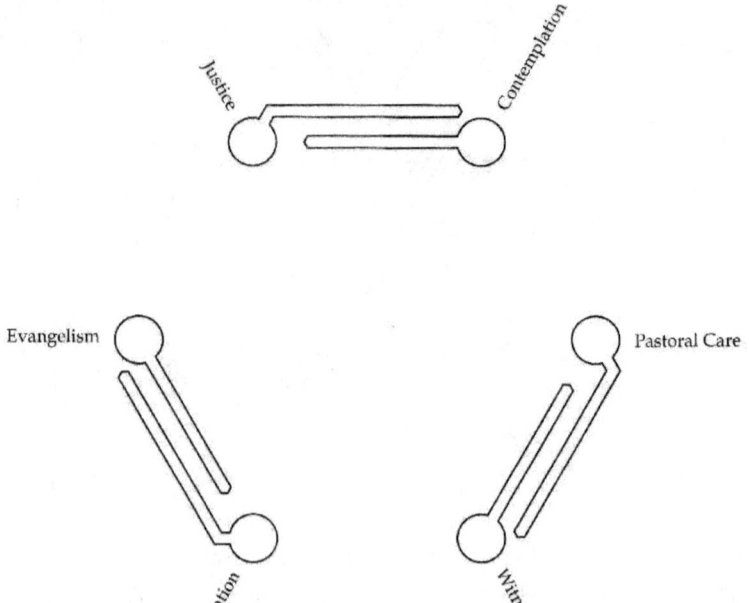

FIGURE 23. Adjacent Ministries, selected so Secondary Ministries will have the maximum diversity.

>    Pastoral Care (S-to-P) and Witness (S-to-W).
>
>    Dedication (W-to-P) and Evangelism (W-to-S).
>
>    Justice (P-to-W) and Contemplation (P-to-S).

The ministries of Pastoral Care and Witness have opposite thrusts. Pastoral Care is a personal ministry, while Witness is impersonal.

The ministries of Dedication and Evangelism have opposite thrusts. Sacred Journey represents a departure into the world and the Open Chalice represents a return from the world.

The ministries of Justice and Contemplation have opposite thrusts. The Dome of Light represents the Holy Spirit outflowing into the world and Sacred Inwardness represents an inflowing into the individual.

**The Mandala of Ministry**

When the two previous illustrations are combined into a single diagram to embrace all the above relationships we get a very beautiful mandala, which forms a vehicle for meditation. (an example of a mandala is given in Figure 24) This mandala shows an interlacing of relationships whose beauty affirms its truth. This diagram is created by superimposing the diagrams shown in Figs. 22 and 23, the diagrams for Opposite and Adjacent Ministries.

FIGURE 24. East meets West. This mandala design was taken from a T-shirt sold to tourists in the markets of Katmandu

Mandala is the Sanskrit word for circle, and mandalas are circular diagrams (figure 24) which are used as aids to meditation and contemplation by focusing the mind and calming the spirit. Each of the six small circles at the perimeter of the mandala shown in Figure 25 represents the primary ministry of a congregation.

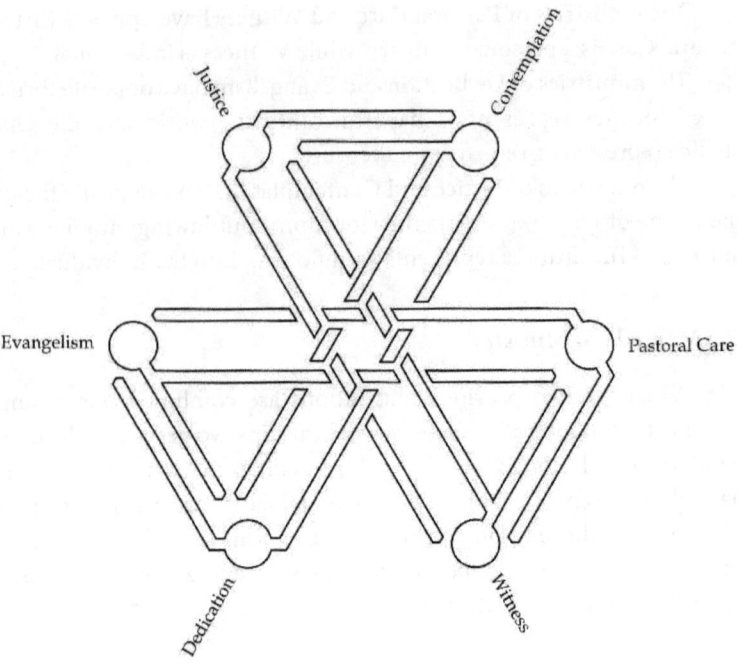

FIGURE 25. Combining the two diagrams for opposite ministries (fig. 22) and adjacent ministries (fig. 23) creates a Mandala where the relationships interlace in the manner of a Celtic Knot pattern. This calm and self-assured diagram contains all the available relationships between ministries.

Two rays emanate from each of these circles and interweave in the manner of a Celtic knot. These rays are links to two secondary purposes which support the primary ministry and round-out the mission of the people. Such a cluster of ministries where a primary ministry is supported by two secondary ministries gives a congregation a very fulfilling mandate; one which materially increases the scope of their worship, and one which probably they would not have chosen for themselves. Looking at each of these relationships in turn, together with an illustration of its trace, we can observe the implications of each of these relationships and see how they enrich congregational worship.

# The Anatomy of Worship

1. Contemplation

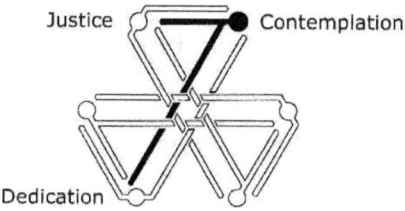

For a congregation that has chosen this transcendental ministry as its primary ministry the two traces from its position on the Mandala cross over the central boundary into the realm of immanence, offering a worldly expansion of its mission. If the worship of a church is purely Contemplation it could hardly be called a church. It needs Dedication in order for it to realize that it is a community. The congregation also needs to take some responsibility for the World they are escaping from; they need to care for Justice. They don't necessarily have to indulge in anything as heroic such as taking on the establishment. Just sending $500 to Greenpeace, working in a food bank, or supporting the environment would do the trick.

2. Pastoral Care

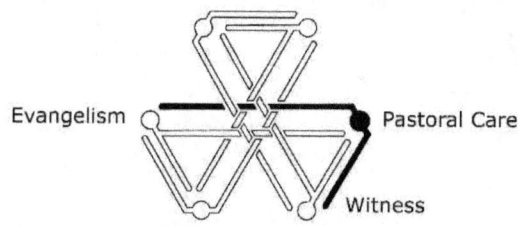

The role of the Mandala is particularly valuable in the case of congregations that, regard Pastoral Care as their primary purpose. These often become focused on their own needs, to the exclusion of anything else. By adopting the ministries of Witness and Evangelism as their secondary purposes they find themselves thrust out into the world, and what could have been a self-centered, self-serving ministry suddenly has to serve the outsider, the stranger.

3. Witness

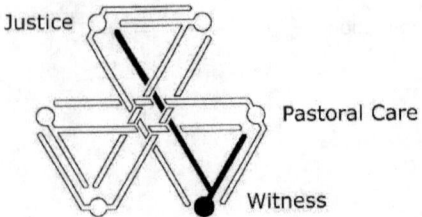

A church whose primary purpose is Witness, being evidence of Christ's presence in the world, can enhance that ministry by caring for the inner needs of its members by supporting healing and reconciliation; by adopting the ministry of Pastoral Care. The Shining is enriched by finding within itself Sacred Meeting; a place for intimacy, care, and support. This can add depth to what could otherwise be quite an impersonal ministry. No adaptations of the building would be necessary to include Justice as a secondary purpose—adding Justice to Witness means we are not only offering the world an ideal, we are also taking responsibility for the way the world is.

4. Dedication

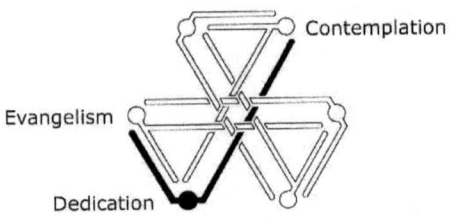

The mandala also stretches the range of those business-oriented congregations that have taken Dedication as their path. Often this ministry is just the translation of a business mind-set into the sphere of worship—a results-oriented spirituality. The mandala will offer true health and salvation to such a community by insisting they enter a world of Contemplation where all their profits and losses are set a zero before the Throne of the Lamb. They also will benefit from the intimate human encounters and warm relationships that Evangelism demands of a community.

## 5. Evangelism

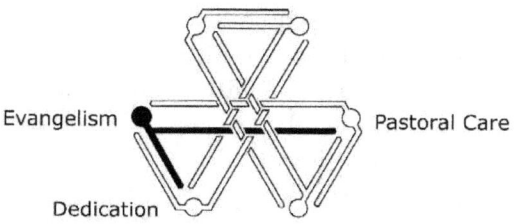

To preserve a continuing community Evangelism needs to be related to Dedication, and to care for its members it needs to undertake Pastoral Care. Many churches who have Evangelism as their primary purpose, notably some Pentecostals and Baptists—suddenly find their ministry is not just about increasing enrolment, they have to care for the people they have enrolled. Sometimes this is not easy for them to do because many of their churches resemble vast movie theatres, and in this form of gathering the audience is passive and has little opportunity for interaction.

## 6. Justice

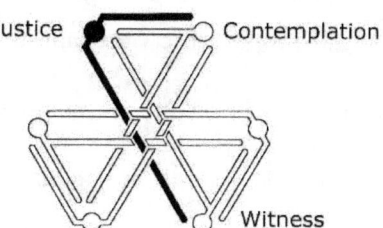

A church whose primary purpose is Justice, advocating peace, freedom, and right livelihood, can enhance its role by adopting the ministry of Witness in which the people acknowledge the role of Christ in what might otherwise be mere politics. In physical terms this might need no more than a banner or a lapel pin. The mission of Justice also needs to be supported by the ministry of Contemplation. The people who are changing the world need a place where they can accept the Unchanging. In the heat of debate they need a place of silence. In their individual strivings they need the strength of community.

Sometimes people might say "Doesn't that restrict us—having to choose a ministry?" In practice I have found the opposite to be the case. When a congregation is unaware of its purpose it tends to worship unconsciously, it tends to worship in the same way day-in and day-out. The style of worship becomes a comfortable habit. This is the true limitation of our freedoms—a restriction that we impose on ourselves because we have not considered that there might be alternatives. In contrast I find that congregations that have adopted the mandala as a touchstone for their devotions experience an increased liveliness, an increased variety, and an enhanced understanding of what they are about.

**Summary of Chapter 3: The Anatomy of Worship**

1. The three parameters of Christian worship are the People, the Sacraments, and the World.
2. Pairing these three parameters yield six possible relationships, each representing a different ministry.
3. The relationship People-to-Sacrament reflects the ministry of Contemplation.
4. The relationship Sacrament-to-People reflects the ministry of Pastoral Care.
5. The relationship Sacrament-to-World reflects the ministry of Witness.
6. The relationship World-to-People reflects the ministry of Dedication.
7. The relationship World-to-Sacrament reflects the ministry of Evangelism.
8. The relationship People-to-World reflects the ministry of Justice.
9. These six ministries express in number, order, and content the six petitions embedded in the Lord's Prayer.
10. To expand the role of congregational worship it is proposed that each of these ministries be supported by a pair of secondary ministries, and a formula is presented to indicate them.

# Chapter 4
# The Great Concordance

In the last chapter we learned that Christian worship can be expressed in exactly six ministries. In this chapter we will discover that each of these ministries can be related to one of Rudolf Schwarz's Six Plans, so a congregation that has chosen its ministry it will know, with precision, how to configure its worship space. We wonder at the possibility that this extraordinary concordance could spring from an underlying world order reflecting a structure for the universe. To support this we find numerous examples in other fields.

**A Structure for Worship**

The six petitions of the Lord's Prayer are framed by a salutation:

"Our Father, who art in Heaven."

and by an acknowledgement:

"for Thine is the Kingdom, the Power, and the Glory, for ever and ever. Amen."

In this prayer the salutation is spoken before the first petition, and the acknowledgement follows the last, but their meaning applies equally to all six petitions, so the salutation and the acknowledgement should not occupy unique positions on the Ring; in fact they are not in themselves petitions but rather they provide a context for each petition on the ring. In the salutation we direct all our petitions to our Heavenly Father, and in the acknowledgement we on earth acknowledge his power to grant them. So each of these petitions is set on its own pathway that extends from earth to heaven. I have indicated this by a three-dimensional structure (see fig 29) which sets our earth below the cycle of petitions and heaven above, in polar positions, with each equatorial petition set between them. The upper and lower poles create an axis around which the ring of prayer revolves.

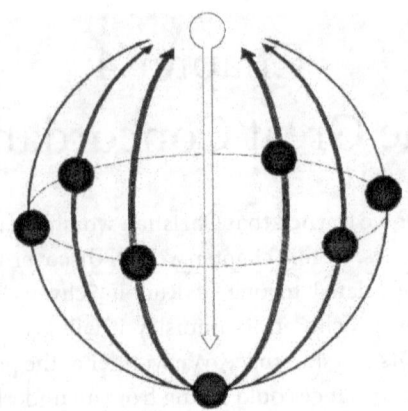

FIGURE 26. A prayer pump. Earth below, Heaven above. Prayers ascend, grace descends

This linking of eight qualities, two of them polar and six of them equatorial, also models a setting for the Cycle of Worship illustrated in Figure 18, page 35, where the six ministries represents the ways in which we worship, and the traces between Heaven and Earth indicate the purpose of our devotions. A flow diagram (figure 26) shows how, like incense, the prayers of each petition ascend to Heaven, and grace descends to the Earth like a gentle dew.

.My use of the terms "polar" and "equatorial" might conjure up an image of a globe, a rotating sphere, with two poles and six equidistant points located on the equator. Euclid's definition of a sphere (Book XI, No 14.) departs from the definition quoted by Plato—"its extremity everywhere equidistant from the center". Euclid chose to define it by the mode of generating it: "When, the diameter of a semicircle remaining fixed, the semicircle is carried round and restored again to the same position from which it began to be moved, the figure so comprehended is a sphere." It could be said that, Euclid's definition is analog, while Plato's is digital.

Euclid's definition includes the concepts of an axis defined by two points, and a rotation; both intrinsic to the structure we have adopted to portray the relationships of worship. The concept of a globe whose rotation ensures that for each continent in turn the sun will be at high noon is an analogy for our conscious attention successively visiting each ministry—a model of our worship. To serve one of my students who was blind I made up a model (figure 27) as an illustration of this three-dimensional structure.

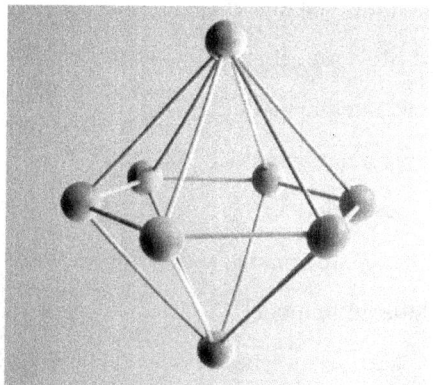

FIGURE 27. A model of the structure of the Our Father. The upper sphere represents Heaven, the lower our Earth, and between them rotate the six petitions of the Lord's Prayer, with six pathways connecting the lower to the upper.

This structure is also a model for the Ring of Plans. We can see support for this when we reflect that the German title for Rudolf Schwarz's book is *Vom Bau der Kirche*, or "from-building-to-church". What transforms a building into a church is the prayers of a worshiping people. Thus if the lower orb represents "building" and the upper orb represents "church" we can see how the worship in each of the orbs representing the Six Plans represents a pathway for this transition. Worship is the force that drives the Plans.

## Models of the Church

Models have always been a useful way of depicting complex relationships. In 1987 James Empereur, who teaches at the Jesuit School of Theology in Berkeley, illustrated a range of liturgies for the church in his work "Models of Liturgical Theology".[25] The cover of his book illustrates the models as seven windows, a happy coincidence because it

---

24. Empereur, *Models*.

implies that the true purpose of a church building is not so much to contain worship as to illuminate it. Empereur lists his liturgies as

A. the Institutional model,

B. the Mystery model,

C. the Sacramental model,

D. the Proclamation model,

E. the Process model,

F. the Therapeutic model, and

G. the Liberation model.

The Institutional and Sacramental models, A and C, have a different quality from the other five in that they represent liturgies, which are ways of worshiping rather than ministries or purposes of worship. Thus the seven models could be grouped as five ministries and two liturgies. Furthermore, when we look at Empereur's descriptions of his models it becomes apparent the Proclamation Model represents a conflation of what we have learned to regard as two separate ministries, those of Witness and Evangelism. Both these ministries involve the parameters of Sacrament and World but in a different order. Witness is expressed in the relationship Sacrament-to-World and Evangelism in World-to-Sacrament. This confusion is widespread as the term Evangelism has been co-opted by the religious right whose practice can be better described as the more impersonal Witness.

Evangelism is essentially a personal relationship, going out into the world and inviting people, one-by-one, to come and share the Feast. Jesus commanded it of his disciples (Luke 10:1) when he appointed seventy-two of his followers and told them to go to every town, two-by-two, and visit people in their homes to share the good news. If they take you in, that's fine. If they don't, just go on to the next town and try again. Witness, in contrast, is not personal. It consists of putting out the word, without really knowing who receives it, as when Jesus preached to large crowds (Matthew 4:23). The situation is further confused because so-called tele-evangelists are in fact operating ministries of Witness. Like the Shopping Channel they send out their messages across the airwaves in the hope that someone will pick them up but they never know who. Because some of these tele-evangelists are exploitive or even criminal, the term evangelism has come into some disrepute—so unfortunate because evangelism is the most intimate, humble, welcoming, and serving ministry of all.

Giving each of these two ministries, Witness and Evangelism, its own place in Empereur's tabulation would give rise to an eightfold array, presenting six ministries and two liturgies. Setting these in the order to which we have become accustomed we see there are obvious correspondences between Empereur's array of models and the Cycle of Worship. Preserving Empereur's nomenclature but revising the order we have:

    1 (B.) The Mystery Model (contemplation)

    2 (F.) The Therapeutic Model (pastoral care)

    3 (D1.) The Proclamation Model (witness)

    4 (E.) The Process Model (dedication)

    5 (D2.) The Proclamation Model (evangelism)

    6 (G.) The Liberation Model (justice)

plus two exclusively liturgical polar models representing earth and heaven:

    (lower) A. The Institutional Model, and

    (upper) C. The Sacramental Model.

Perhaps the linkage between The Process Model and the Ministry of Dedication needs a word of explanation. Rooted in the work of Alfred North Whitehead[26], process theology postulates that God is present in the world, and in an ever-changing world God too is changed, and our worship is a work in progress directed more to the future than to the past. Process theology honors our work in the world as the world is the arena for God's working in our lives. This is the foundation of the Ministry of Dedication where the World is a path for the People. The tabulation points up the clarity that comes from combining pairs of parameters to create the Cycle of Worship (figure 18). It provides a conceptual framework where some earlier models can find their place, and indicates

---

25. Whitehead, *Process and Reality*.

where there are some gaps in their systems. It clarifies definitions where some disparate ministries have been fused together; and it separates out those church activities that we should not regard as worship.

| James Empereur (7 liturgies) | this work (6 ministries, 2 poles) | |
|---|---|---|
| The Mystery Model | 1 Contemplation | P-to-S |
| The Therapeutic Model | 2 Pastoral Care | S-to-P |
| The Proclamation Model | 3 Witness | S-to-W |
| The Process Model | 4 Dedication | W-to-P |
| Proclamation (duplicate) | 5 Evangelism | W-to-S |
| The Liberation Model | 6 Justice | P-to-W |
| The Institutional Model | (south) Earth | |
| The Sacramental Model | (north) Heaven | |

FIGURE 28. Correspondences: In the first column a listing of the models of James Empereur. The worship supported by these models is listed in the second column.

**An Eternal World Order**

We have seen expressions of a six-fold structure for worship. Six entities rotate about an axis established by an additional pair. They are:

1. The Cycle of Worship, based on its three parameters.

2. The ordering of the petitions in the Our Father.

3. James Empereur's Models of Liturgical Theology.

These six-fold arrays are all similar in form to the layout of the Ring of Plans based on the insights of Rudolf Schwarz, but that similarity could spring from a bias imposed by our Judeo-Christian heritage. To establish that space and worship are intrinsically linked we would have to identify an underlying world order that is eternal and cross-cultural. We would have to establish that our discovery of six spinning spheres, like the ring-bound six arms and legs of the dancing Shiva Nataraja (figure 29) is an exemplar of a structure for the universe.

THE CLEVELAND MUSEUM OF ART : THE WADE COLLECTION

FIGURE 29. Shiva Nataraja—The Eternal Dance

## A secular six-fold structure

I came across an example of such a structure by accident. I was on my way to class at Trinity College and feeling pretty good because I really love teaching, when I noticed that Book City had a display of newly-published books in their window. The title of one of them—"The World in Six Songs"—jumped out at me. The "six" in the title caught my eye, just as it had been caught thirty years previously by Simone Weil's exposition on the six petitions in the Our Father. I had just been musing on whether the world could have a six-fold structure, and here were the words "world" and "six" coming together in the title of a book[27]. I did not have time to read the book before class so I just skimmed through it. From the dust jacket I gathered that the author, Daniel J. Levitin, is a neuroscientist at McGill University and a former music producer with some gold records to his credit. His thesis is that music has been with humans since we first became human. It has shaped our world through six kinds of songs: songs of friendship, joy, comfort, knowledge, religion, and love.

In my class "Shaping Space for Worship" I wrote out in a circle the titles which Daniel Levitin had given to his Six Songs.

*friendship*     *joy*

*love*                    *comfort*

*religion*     *knowledge*

Without prompting all the students immediately noted the similarities between the six songs and the cycle of six ministries, they felt it was an extraordinary correspondence, and so did I.

When I finally got to read Daniel Levitin's book I found his thesis is that songs have had an adaptive role in evolution; that they have aided our survival, and thus they have shaped our world. So songs of friendship, as he defines them, have a role in social bonding to create a secure society where our chances of survival will be enhanced. His illustrations of songs of friendship include such numbers as Bruce Cockburn's "If I had a rocket launcher" based on Pete Seeger's "If I had a hammer", and "We shall overcome!"—a key anthem of the US civil rights

---

26. Levitin: The World in Six Songs.

movement. Thus friendship songs have a definite connection with the ministry of justice. Perhaps comradeship would be a more accurate title for this class of songs because it evokes a common purpose—but friendship is a more appealing word.

Similarly, Daniel sees love songs as being adaptive when they express a tenderness between parents which helps establish stable families for raising children. Love, beyond just sex, promotes the growth of the human family, just as evangelism promotes the growth of the church. He added the insight that all our ancestors were raised with such loving care that none of them suffered from infant mortality. Songs shape the evolution of our humanity just as space shapes the liturgy of our worship.

The remaining categories of song show a more obvious correspondence. "Joy" reflects the adoration of a People gathered around a Sacrament. "Comfort" reflects the healing the Sacrament bestows on the People. "Knowledge" is imparted by the preaching function of Witness. "Religion" and Dedication are almost synonymous, and already we have seen how Evangelism is founded on "Love". Justice is secured by dedicated "Friends" going out into the world.

I was struck that the order in which Dr. Levitin presented his six songs was the same as the order in which I had set the six ministries, so taking advantage of the fact that, unlike St. Augustine, this author was still alive, I asked him "What induced you to set out the Six Songs in that order?"

He graciously replied "This was purely a narrative decision, not a scientific or pedagogical one."

That was music to my ears. Narrative implies the telling of a story which has an internal flow and order. Like music it implies a succession of phrases where each leads to the next, just like the Cycle of Worship.

Getting back to Daniel Levitin I asked "And why did you start the list with Friendship, particularly as on page 84 of your book two famous songwriters, Sting and Rodney Crowell, mention they thought that the first songs would be songs of Joy." (Joy would have corresponded to Contemplation, which was the first entry in my catalogue). "Same reason" was the reply. "I hope that helps."

However, the starting point for the cycle is not important as long as the order remains intact, because the implied rotation will let each entity occupy a prime position in due course. The songs rotate between the twin poles of the singer and the listener—in the case of songs of "Joy" these two might be the same person. This structure duplicates with precision the Cycle of Worship, but there is nothing inherently religious in the structural disposition of the six songs. This points to an underlying universal order that unites them both: an affinity that enables us to create spaces that can participate in worship.

**Shaping Space for Worship**

We have identified six instances of a thought pattern where eight quantities are arranged so that two of them form an axis for the rotation of the remaining six. They are:

1. The Ring of Plans

2. The Cycle of Nature

3. The Cycle of Worship

4. Lord's Prayer petitions

5. James Empereur's liturgical models

6. Daniel Levitin's Six Songs

This pattern has shown up in many divers fields. The universality of this cosmological construct offers two possibilities, both of them profound: either this is the way God created the world, or this is the way our minds are attuned so as to be able to perceive it. Schwarz himself supported this view[28], saying "The sequence of the plans was established not by accident but rather by the very structure of creation itself—and this indeed is not an accident, it is the revealed form of eternity in time."

The value of this thought pattern is that it makes possible relationships between entities in many different fields, based on their occupying corresponding positions in their arrays. This is supported by the Platonic maxim[29] "like knows like"; stating that in order for a material entity to be perceived a corresponding mental form must first exist in the mind. Thus we can postulate a structural relationship between

---

27. Schwarz, Church Incarnate, 193.

28. Cornford, Plato's Cosmology, 65.

# The Great Concordance

The Ring of Six Plans and The Cycle of Six Ministries. They are fed by the same underground source, they emerge from the same foundation, even though the Six Plans were conceived in a mystical vision and the six ministries were generated by mathematical calculation.

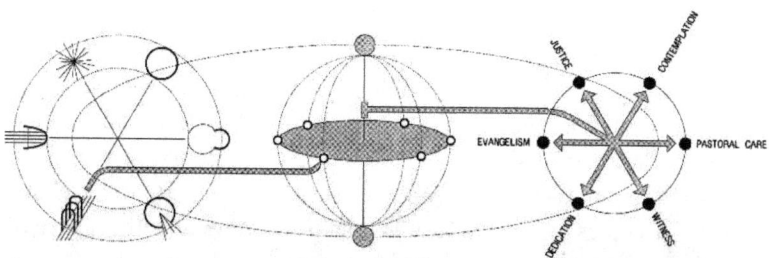

FIGURE 30. Linked Systems. A universal principle (center) finds spatial expression in the Ring of Plans and temporal expression in the Cycle of Worship. This systemic translation enables any of the Plans on the Ring to support all the Ministries of the Church.

This universal structure is represented in the central diagram of Figure 30. It's six elements find spatial expressions in the diagram on the left, where we see how Rudolf Schwarz's Six Plans enable six buildings to develop into their role as churches. The right-hand diagram is a temporal expression of the same universal structure. Here we see how the layout of the whole system may be expressed by the Cycle of Worship. In this diagram, which is independent of space, all six ministries may coexist so individual ministries may be invoked in any order as rotation brings each one into prominence. From this we can deduce that each of the Six Plans can house all the expressions of worship.

By this token we see that each ministry of the Christian church can find its expression not only in prayer, study, song, and praise, but also in the consciously-shaped space of the vessel that contains it. From this we can deduce that space, as a verb, also worships.

Space has the capacity to worship, and to share its worship with us. Emerson said "I like the silent church before the service begins, better than any preaching"[30], and many who visit ancient sacred

---

29. Emerson, Self-Reliance.

sites have felt that the prayers of past generations are still being offered in these places; the spirit has become embedded in the stones. . In a sense, we have become part of that ancient community of worshipers, and we can join our worship with them. Space can pray, and now that we have learned how to configure spaces so they are able to express worship we can join with them in our worship.

Thus by adopting one of the Six Plans a congregation can shape a space that will support and symbolize its worship. By discovering its purpose a congregation wishing to build a new church will know which of the Six Plans it should adopt to order its space. It should select the Plan that occupies the same position on the Ring of Plans as its chosen ministry occupies on the Cycle of Worship. We have seen that space is a fluid thing, subject to our will, and it has powers of expression that can assist us in our worship. That said, an undefined or purpose-less space has the capacity to frustrate and inhibit worship. It is unfortunate that most worship spaces manage to do just that. After visiting and studying over a thousand churches I have come to the conclusion that when a worship space is aligned with one of the Six Plans it evokes feelings of peace, calm, purposefulness, and integrity. When we visit a place of worship whose planning is not based on a ministry, or is based on aspects of several different ministries, we find confusion and irritation. It is as if we cannot find a gestalt for the place; we can't understand it; it has no sense of wholeness, it sends us mixed messages. In attempting to get our heads around such a space we expend energy and experience a confusion which makes worship difficult. So it is of vital importance for a community to select one of the Six Plans as a guiding principle for configuring its worship space.

It is not difficult for a congregation to define its ministry. Most congregations have adopted a mission statement to define themselves, to focus on their purpose, and to present themselves to the world. In fact this is why the congregation exists; for community worship by mutual alignment and consent. Even the most self-congratulatory mission statement—high-flown phrases expressing noble sentiments—can be analyzed to determine which of the six ministries comes closest to defining its choice for worship; a choice which can then be supported by selecting the corresponding Plan. This plan will then be a constant reminder to the community of the role it has chosen as its mission. Each Plan has characteristics that support the relationship of parameters implicit in its corresponding ministry. These characteristics are listed for each Plan on pages 4 and 5, and will be considered in more detail in the following chapters where we study examples of how the Plans have been realized in built form. The list of characteristics for each Plan does not claim to be exhaustive; I have extracted just enough features to be useful. By contemplating the Plans and by a careful reading Schwarz's book we may discover other possibilities for expression.

A different situation may exist when a congregation wishes to renovate an existing church. They may find that the building they have inherited does not express the ministry they have adopted as their mission. For example, a church with a long narrow nave would find it difficult to express any ministry other than Dedication unless the congregation were prepared to indulge in widespread demolition. Sir Christopher Wren had this luxury in 1668 when he used gunpowder to bring down an old Gothic cathedral in order to build the new St. Paul's Cathedral. Unfortunately he got too enthusiastic with his detonations and one of his charges bombarded his neighbors with flying brick, stones, and rubble. Thereafter he had to cool his jets and resort to the more conservative battering rams.

Few of us will have the opportunity to renovate on so dramatic a scale. Most of us will need to adopt a more sensitive approach. When we have inherited an existing church, as did Sir Christopher Wren, we will need to listen to what the stones are saying. We should try to identify the Plan which comes closest to the existing structure—the one that could be achieved with a minimum of disruption. Then we must do whatever disrupting is needed! We must enhance all those features which support that Plan and purge those features that compromise it. It is a paradox that buildings, those things which we feel to be solid and unmovable are in fact malleable—it is always possible to make windows a little bit smaller or doors a little bit wider until one plan mutates into the next. On the other hand ministries are definitions and are therefore immutable. It may take courage to do the work that needs to be done: the courage to brick up windows, open new entrances, level floors, move seating, change focus, deploy new lighting, and convene a yard sale of left-over holy hardware. But there will be a huge surge of energy in knowing that this is being done for a higher purpose. This work will release a flow of universal energy which previously had been blocked.

When we model our space on one of the Plans we experience a release of energy that will permeate our space and energize our worship. This energy flows from the source of all energy, a Universal Principle of which the Ring of Plans is an expression. Each of the Six Plans is associated with a unique expression of ministry, and because we have established mathematically that there are exactly six unique ministries it follows that there are exactly six Plans—Schwarz would be surprised! This is the expression of a Universal Principle in which the infinite becomes finite, the universal become individualized, and we can see what was previously invisible.

This Universal Principle also finds expression the Cycle of Worship with its six rotating ministries, so the shared universal foundation unites the Cycle of Worship and the Ring of Plans. In this relationship we are uniting not just particular plans with particular ministries—we are relating whole systems. Thus each Plan, by virtue of being found on the Ring of the Six Plans which relates to the Cycle of Worship, is related to all of the Six Ministries, and each individual Plan is able to be a venue for all the six forms of worship.

The Cycle of Worship rotates rapidly, as rapidly as we can voice one prayer to follow another. In the words of Herbert O'Driscoll, taken from his Foreword: "Worship is a jewel that turns unceasingly, offering now this color and now that, responding now to this aspect of the human-divine encounter and now that."

The rotation of ministries round an axis created by "the human-divine encounter" means time must be a dimension in our model. This gives us, within the system, freedom at different times to worship in different ways. The connection we are forging is not just the simplistic association of one plan with one ministry; it is a bonding of systems. So any given Plan, being part of a system of Plans, can be a vehicle for all the ministries represented in the Cycle of Worship, as shown in Figure 30, page 61. It can be a vessel for all worship, even the worship of those ministries it was not specifically designed to support. The converse of this is: a building that is not based on one of the Six Plans will not be able to support any worship, as it would have no connection with the Cycle of Worship; and we have found that this Cycle embraces all possible ministries. So it is essential to make the space in our building become an expression of one of the Six Plans.

## The Work

The concordance between the Cycle of Worship and the Ring of Plans is an expression of a universal principle. This convergence gives us tools to craft both a congregation's worship and its worship space in a way that will promote its wellbeing and support its ministry. The Cycle of Worship assists congregations in choosing their primary ministry by providing a finite list of options. Most congregations have already made their choice in this matter, but the debate itself is often a useful source of clarity.

The Mandala which is derived from the Cycle of Worship directs a congregation to adopt a further pair of choices, perhaps unlikely ones, for a pair of secondary ministries. These are choices which, without a bit of prompting, they might have avoided. Nevertheless these are the choices calculated to make church life more vital by encouraging it to expand in unforeseen directions. In my experience, once a congregation has accepted a primary ministry they have little objection to exploring the implications of expanding that ministry. Often they are agreeable, or even enthused, to embark on a journey of discovery, not knowing where the journey is going to end, but at least they are in agreement on their starting point and they know that they are on the right road.

## A Beautiful Symmetry

Here is a beautiful symmetry. Each of the Six Plans in Rudolf Schwarz's array serves a distinct form of worship.

This inspired the analysis of worship in chapter 3, the Anatomy of Worship, which discovered that all worship may be expressed in exactly six ministries.

A linkage deduced in chapter 4, The Great Concordance, revealed that these six ministries (as there are no others) must be the responses to the Six Plans.

This adds a mathematical precision to Rudolf Schwarz's original intuition in creating his Six Plans.

## Building with the Plans

The Ring of Plans offers an appropriate model for those congregations building a new worship space, and a feasible model for those engaging in reordering an existing worship space. If the spatial requirements for ministry can be presented with clarity and respect, then the optimal form of the proposed worship space can be developed by the congregation in an atmosphere of agreement.

Examples, listed on the "Contents" page, of how this has been worked out in practice are given in the following six chapters. These show how worship spaces have been shaped to support each of the six ministries of the church. These are not examples to be copied, but rather they should be regarded as expressions of a universal principle. To repeat the beautiful words of Rudolf Schwarz: "The Plans are a happening that has withdrawn utterly into its potentiality, which has become entirely seed and beginning, and which waits, not to be copied, but to grow up once more as new."

In these examples we will see how space links with worship in a universal harmony. Stones and the Spirit embrace each other.

**Summary of Chapter 4: The Great Concordance**

1. The six ministries of the Christian church may be represented as occurring in a circular array which rotates about an axis defined by two more quantities. Six examples of arrays with such a structure are given, taken from sources that are pre-Christian, Christian, and secular. Such examples may be considered as outcroppings of a universal world order

2. This universal world order has a space-based expression in the Six Plans of Rudolf Schwarz and a time-based expression in the Cycle of Worship. This concordance allows space to worship, and by this to support our worship.

3. Worship is the expression of a relationship between a People and a Sacrament. Ministry is a duty which a congregation accepts. Each of the six ministries may be supported by any one of the Six Plans, thus the space formed by each of the Six Plans has a sacred purpose. This purpose imparts a sacred quality to the space, and this quality enables a space to support all worship.

4. A congregation may embrace several ministries. It may do this because ministries may be separated in time. Space, however, exists

outside of time, it is eternal, so a congregation's worship may be independent of the expression of its worship space.

5. Thus any church based on one of the Six Plans can support all six expressions of worship.

6. In the following six chapters examples are given to show how each of the Six Plans has been realized in practice, both for building new churches and for renewing existing ones, as follows:

# Chapter 5: The First Plan *for* the Ministry of Contemplation

**The First Communion**

The first Eucharist took place in an upper room in an ordinary house. The room did not have to be especially large—just adequate for a dinner party with thirteen guests, and perhaps space for two or three others to serve the food. There would be an ordinary table or bench to carry the food, and as the Last Supper took place after sundown, the table would have candles or an oil lamp on it for illumination. There would have to be a cup for the wine and perhaps some baskets for the bread, and bowls for the rest of the food.

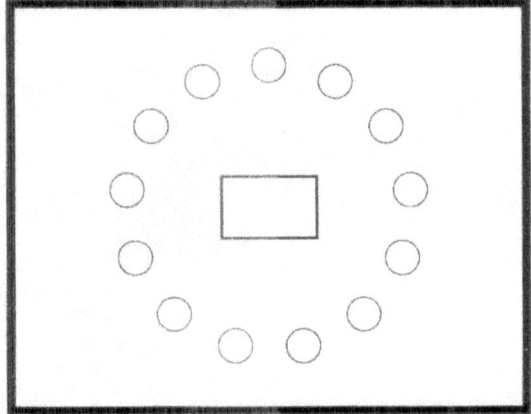

FIGURE 31. Anatomy of the Last Supper: Thirteen friends in an Upper Room share a meal.

The thirteen dinner guests sat in a circle with the lamplight shining on their faces, their backs to the walls of the room. The walls would have to be strong because this was a time of great political unrest. Even though the moon was approaching its full it was not safe to be out at night. Armed gangs were roaming the streets, various sects were vying for

# The First Plan

influence, the various religious authorities were struggling to maintain their supremacy, and the secular authority oppressed them all.

The walls united to form a strong ring to keep this struggle at a distance so those who were at peace with one another could experience peace in the safety of the upper room. One of the guests who did not have peace in his heart found this offer of serenity to be intolerable. He had been personally and uniquely offered food by the Master. He knew how much was being offered to him and how little he was able to accept. He had to leave the gathering, forgiven in advance for the chain of events he was about to set in motion.

Outside there was violence and betrayal, but the walls preserved the inner peace. The remaining twelve guests shared the first Eucharist in Sacred Inwardness—an Inwardness in which we can all share.

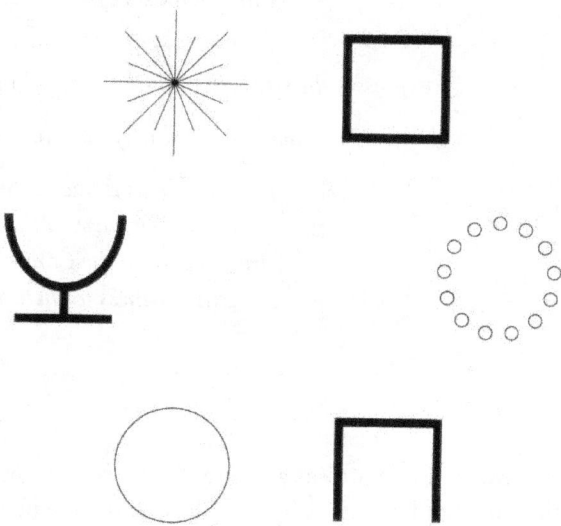

FIGURE 32. The Elements of the First Eucharist, and all subsequent Eucharists: space, community, table, bread, cup, and light—each of these elements has become a powerful symbol, enriching our experience of the Eucharist.

## Sacred Inwardness

*The table is in the center of the space.*
*The worshipers gather around it.*
*The children, and the very old, those especially loved, are in the front.*

*Candles on the table light the faces of all around,*
*They focus their attention on the Feast.*
*They share the Peace with one another.*
*Their relationship is warm and human;*
*they are members of the Body of Christ.*

*The ring in which they are seated*
*expresses the strength of the bonds that unite them,*

*While facing inward they also face each other.*

*Their focus is Sacred Inwardness;*
*Inwardness to the Eucharist,*
*Inwardness to the Community, and*
*Inwardness to their own Being.*

Sacred Inwardness expresses a central focus, away from the walls. The walls that surround this space have no decoration or embellishment. They arch over the space to form a dome, white and featureless. The dome surrounds the space, contains it, and keeps it safe. The dome is not disturbed by chaos and hostility outside. It creates a totally internal serenity.

THE FIRST PLAN

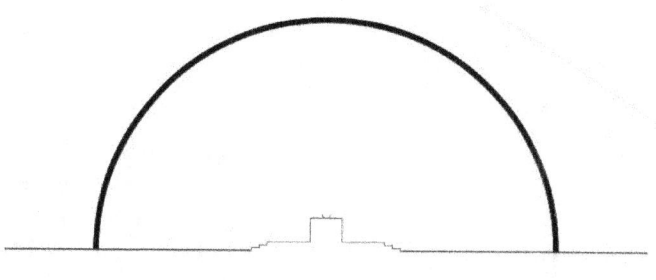

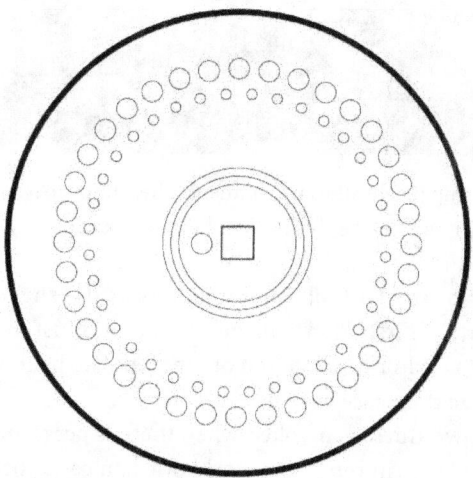

FIGURE 33. The First Plan: Sacred Inwardness, for the ministry of Contemplation.

The opposite pole of inner serenity is outer turmoil. The dome would be redundant if peace prevailed in the world. This form of building is appropriate when the church is located in a hostile environment. In Sarajevo, that crucible of European unrest, the congregation of the Church of the Assumption of the Blessed Virgin Mary (figure 34) meet and worship in the bombed-out shell of their former church.

FIGURE 34. Worship in a hostile environment. The Church of the Assumption of the Blessed Virgin in Stup, a suburb of Sarajevo in Bosnia.

The umbrellas of the faithful are miniatures of the sheltering dome of Rudolf Schwarz's First Plan. Imagine what it must be like for the congregation to huddle under a roof of umbrellas, to hear distant gunfire, and to exchange the Peace with one another.

Sacred Inwardness is invoked when there is persecution or natural danger outside. The church in the world of Islam could be built like this, or the church in the desert, or the church which found it necessary to hide itself away in the dark of the Catacombs. When we build a church for Sacred Inwardness it is both an expression of our lives and an indictment of our times. It bears witness to the difficulties we experience in the world—the hurts, the temptations, the distractions, the failures. It is therefore an appropriate form to enclose the worship of those contemplative orders that find the world intolerable; that feel they must reject the world in order to pursue inner peace.

Ultimately, there is a sadness in this form of building. The seed is in the earth and the earth is dark. No matter how pure the inner serenity there is threaded through it the knowledge that in rejecting the world we are ourselves rejected. The Body of Christ is in the Tomb. We wait, fearfully.

# The First Plan

## The First Church

The first Church building that we know of, that is, the first building that was built specifically for Christian worship, is the Old Church at Glastonbury, built in 64 AD This church was built by twelve missionaries sent over from Gaul by the Apostle St. Philip. Tradition says that their number included St. Joseph of Arimathaea. Their boat made landfall at the Isle of Avalon, close to Glastonbury. In 1125 William of Malmesbury[31] wrote:

> "There are documents of no small credit, which have been discovered in certain places to the following effect, that no other hands than those of the Disciples of Christ erected the church at Glastonbury. By these was built the ancient church of St. Mary of Glastonbury, as faithful tradition has handed down through decaying time."

To build the church the missionaries first dug a series of holes in a circle 39.6 feet in diameter. Saplings were set in these holes, and laced together overhead to form a dome. This church "of wandes and branches" was used for worship for hundreds of years. It was regularly tended and maintained by monks, pilgrims and visitors, and stood foremost among the sacred spaces of Europe. There is a record of Paulinus, Bishop of Rochester, repairing the roof of the church when it was already over five hundred years old. This structure, so old and so revered, was replaced by a stone building after a fire in 1184, but in such a way as to preserve the original dimensions. The dimensions were still available because the foundations consisted of a ring of holes, and in archeology the hardest thing to destroy is a hole. A stone can be moved, but it's not possible to move a hole. If the hole contains a wooden post, the wood as it rots away creates a different chemical composition. If the post is removed and the hole is filled-in the filling has a different density and composition, and this can be detected thousands of years later.

---

30. William of Malmesbury, *Chronicles*.

ST. MARY'S CHAPEL, GLASTONBURY ABBEY.

FIGURE 35. The Mary Chapel, Glastonbury, built on the site of the first Christian church. The carved molding at the corner could be a depiction of a surveyor's rod or measuring staff, inviting one to measure the temple and learn the significance of its dimensions. The photograph is the frontispiece to the Rev. Lionel Smithett Lewis's "St. Joseph of Arimathaea at Glastonbury, or The Apostolic Church in Britain" 1922.

The Mary Chapel (figure 35), the stone structure that replaced the Old Church, was built in a rectangular shape 39.6 feet wide and 68.6 feet long. In this proportion the diagonal is equal to exactly twice the length of the shorter side. Any master mason of the time would know that such a proportion could be contained in a regular hexagon (figure 36) or a six-pointed star (the Mogen David) and an inscribed circle of 39.6 feet diameter would just fit inside such a star. Thus the "new" stone structure embodies the space and size of the original church by embracing an equal internal area and by equating its width to the original diameter.

# The First Plan

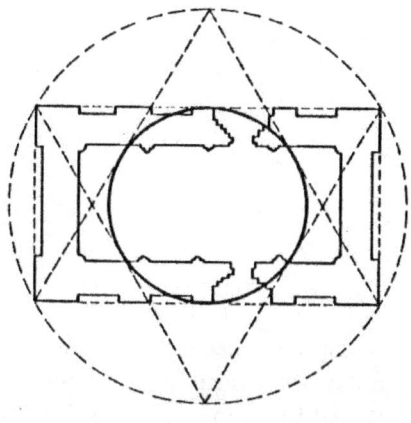

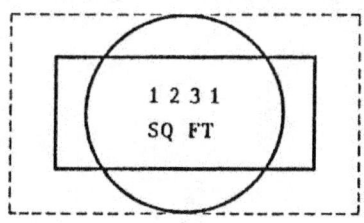

FIGURE 36. The upper diagram combines two versions of the Mary Chapel at Glastonbury. The small inner circle represents the original circular wooden oratory, said to be built by the disciples of Christ. A six-pointed star mediates between the original dimensions of this oratory and the stone structure that replaced it in 1184. The drawing was adapted from John Michell's "City of Revelation"[32]. The lower diagram shows how the two structures were built to enclose equal areas, so the old is contained in the new.

So the original church was quite tiny. With an area of 1,231 square feet it could comfortably contain one hundred worshipers, so the original twelve missionaries must have anticipated at least an eightfold increase in their numbers. Sacred Inwardness would have been an appropriate form of worship for this first

---

31. Michell, City of Revelation, 45.

congregation. It would provide security from present dangers and future upheavals. Too, some of the Church Builders would remember the Sacred Inwardness they had experienced personally at the Last Supper.

**The Shape of Worship**

By building a domed ceiling or a circular plan we do not automatically create Sacred Inwardness—this derives from a ring of worshipers surrounding a sacrament. It is the shape of worship that is important rather than the shape of the building. A round building can certainly support a congregation meeting in Sacred Inwardness, in fact it does this better than any other form, but it cannot on its own create Sacred Inwardness. Sacred Inwardness is not a shape or a mood; it is a form for a worshiping community. Two examples, two paradoxes, will illustrate this: a cruciform church that accommodates the centralized worship of Sacred Inwardness, and a circular church that does not.

THE FIRST PLAN

## St. Mark's Catholic Church, Burlington, Vermont.
Freeman, French, and Freeman, Architects. 1944.

St. Mark's Catholic Church was built out of a willingness to re-examine the traditions of the Mass: to retain what is eternal and to be prepared to change that which is not. This was in the 1940s, twenty years before Vatican II blew a breath of fresh air through the Catholic Church. In those days every catholic altar was built up against the end wall of the church, and the priest celebrating Mass had his back to the people. The people could not see what he was doing; they had to take it on faith.

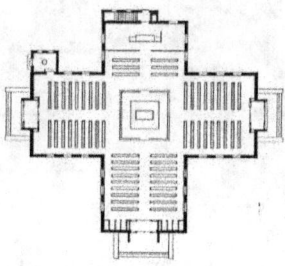

FIGURE 37. Plan of St. Mark's Church, Burlington, Vermont, showing the central placement of the altar.

Father Tennien of St. Mark's Church saw no reason why the people could not have a more involving role in the Mass, and he proposed the radical step of bringing the altar into the center of the church. This farout idea was reported in TIME magazine[33] under the heading "*An Early Christian Altar*": "St. Mark's Roman Catholic Church at Burlington, Vermont, a gleaming structure of glass blocks and red brick, and designed by local architects who were chosen because they had never designed a Catholic Church before, is strictly 20th Century. But it has one primitive feature that has rarely been seen in Christian churches since the 9th Century. Its altar is set in the center of the church so that the face and hands of the priest offering Mass are visible to his congregation from three sides."

---

32. TIME Magazine, August 7th 1944, 46.

EZRA STOLLER, ESTO PHOTO

FIGURE 38. In the foursquare St. Mark's Catholic Church the worshipers are gathered in the form of a ring around the altar.

The people sit in a ring around the altar (figure 37), a square ring rather than a round one, but a ring nevertheless, and they witness the Mass from three sides. The architects contained this seating arrangement in three rectangular volumes, and by adding a fourth for the choir and sacristy they created a traditional cruciform plan as a vessel for an innovative arrangement for worship in the mode of Sacred Inwardness.

Thus Sacred Inwardness devolves from the focus of a worshiping congregation. It does not follow automatically from the disposition of the walls of a building. The next example we will study is a church which has circular walls but does not support the ministry of Sacred Inwardness.

THE FIRST PLAN

## L'Eglise de Notre Dame de France, 5 Leicester Place, London.
Hector O. Corfiato, Architect, 1953.

This is a completely circular church (figure 39) without any windows. From these statements one might deduce that the congregation worshiped in Sacred Inwardness, but such is not the case. The church is just off Leicester Square in the theatre district of London. It was originally a theatrical building for the display of "panoramas". These were images painted on its cylindrical walls and viewed from a system of platforms in the center—the Victorian precursor of the wrap-around screen.

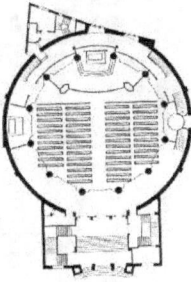

FIGURE 39. Plan of L'Eglise de Notre Dame de France, London. An inherited circular plan has no influence on the form of worship.

In 1865 the building was converted into a church for French Catholics, and was much used by French service men and women in the war. It was bombed in the war, and rebuilt in 1953. It has a notable mural by Jean Cocteau with strong and strange Rosicrucian overtones, depicting a crucifixion that is being ignored by all the bystanders including the artist whose self-portrait is included in the crowd. It has been revealed that Jean Cocteau[34], beside his public life as a poet, artist, and cinematographer, had a private role as Grand Master of the Prieuré de Sion, or Priory of Zion, an ancient and secret order devoted to Grand restoring the Merovignian monarchy to the thrones of Europe. Previous Masters of the Order included the alchemist Nicolas Flanel, Sir Isaac Newton, Charles Radclyffe, Victor Hugo, and Claude Debussy. The

---

33. Baigent et al. Holy Blood and the Holy Grail, 161–4.

Prieuré de Sion, with Jewish and Christian influences, traces the Merovignian lineage back to Jesus; so the crowd, and the artist, by looking away from the cross into the distance, could support the thesis that Jesus' bloodline, if not his life, did not end at the crucifixion but continued, perhaps into the Merovingnian Dynasty.

FIGURE 40. In the completely circular L'Eglise de Notre Dame de France the seating is on the square, showing that the shape of a building is not necessarily the same as the shape of its worship.

The Prieuré de Sion was a secular sponsor of the Knights Templar and has links with Freemasonry and the Rosicrucians. In witness to this, in Cocteau's mural there is at the foot of the cross a large rose-cross medallion.

The church is not sure whether it should regard this work as an artistic treasure or an embarrassing apostasy. When I visited the church the curé was doubtful about letting me see the mural until I explained in transatlantic French that I was "un canadien errant" and then it was O.K.

The circular form of this church was inherited from its original theatrical use rather than from any pattern of worship of the congregation. In fact the pattern of worship follows a traditional linear form with a raised altar at one end of the space and parallel rows of pews, just as one might find in a thousand traditional churches. However, one can wonder that perhaps an expression of Sacred Inwardness might have been a very appropriate symbol for the worship of expatriate French people in London.

**Building with the Plan**

An illustration of the First Plan is presented in Figure 33, page 71. However it would probably be unwise for a congregation to attempt to build a church using this illustration as their plan. The Fire Marshall would have some comments on the lack of exits, and the congregation would have some comments on the lack of washrooms. The purpose of the illustration is to show the relationships of Sacred Inwardness and the qualities of space that support that ministry. It is these qualities that we must capture in an architectural plan if it is to be an embodiment of the First Plan.

Three examples follow, to show how this has been accomplished. The qualities they take from the First Plan are:

> a single spatial volume,
>
> strong walls, and
>
> a central altar.

The three examples that follow show buildings that are very different, even though they all embody the qualities of Sacred Inwardness. As all the plans in this book are drawn to the same scale you can readily see that the ministry of contemplation can find expression in some of the largest and in some of the smallest buildings which are illustrated in the following pages.

## Founders' Chapel, Wycliffe College, Toronto.
### G. M. Miller, Architect, 1891.

In the Founders' Chapel one feels that the outside world is being held at a distance. Strong walls preserve the peace, and the high windows of heavily painted stained glass admit little light. There are no doors to the exterior; access is by a labyrinthine corridor—an underground passage—which connects to the adjacent College buildings (figure 41).

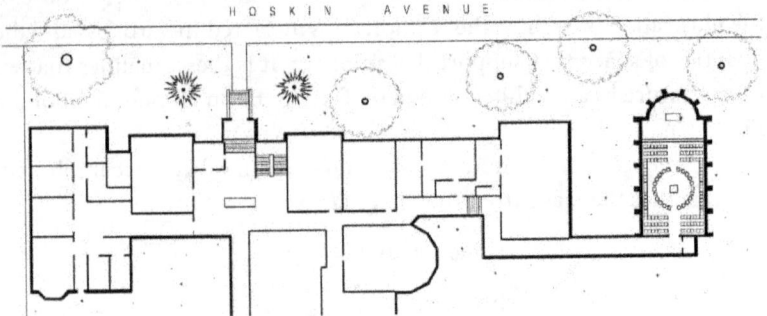

FIGURE 41. At Wycliffe College in Toronto the Founders' Chapel, seen on the right, is sited as remote from the entrance as it could possibly be, safe from all outside influences.

Such a tortuous entry way is in itself a defense against the stranger, requiring that he enter the College by the front door (seen on the left side of the illustration), traverse the lobby, follow the east corridor through the classroom wing and at the entrance to the refectory descend a flight of stairs to a lower level which gives access to a winding "underground passage", in order to arrive at the Chapel.

FIGURE 42. For an evangelical community a contemplative worship space. Founders' Chapel shows how the Ring of Plans can generate spaces to support all Christian worship.

In this quiet womb-like interior one can feel totally safe, a perfect venue for the Ministry of Contemplation. Recently, movable chairs were installed, replacing the old wooden pews, so the seating could be arranged for centralized worship as seen in Figure 42. However the chairs are usually to be found arranged in the same straight rows as the old pews they replaced.

The form of Founders' Chapel is an accurate reflection of the mindset of the founders of Wycliffe College, which was conceived as a defensive bulwark in a time of hostility. In 1882 in Toronto political power was shifting from an earlier aristocracy to a rising class of merchants and industrialists. These self-made men were suspicious of the pomp and hierarchy of the Anglican Church under the leadership of Bishop John Strachan, and in reaction against the Romish practices and false doctrine which they perceived in the Trinity College which the

Bishop had founded they established their own theological college on Hoskin Avenue.

Some of this spirit of hostility and resentment has seeped into the stones, and even today a leaven of malice requires an on-going vigilance to keep it in check. The prospects for peace were not helped when in 1925 the Liberal-Catholic Anglican Trinity College moved into new premises across the street from Wycliffe.

Wycliffe College describes itself as being in the Evangelical Reformation Tradition of the Anglican Church, with a low-church focus on preaching and personal salvation, so it is ironic that its worship space should be such a perfect space for Contemplation, a ministry which is probably low on its list of priorities. However, any attempt to make the space more cognizant of the sinful world outside by opening up doors and windows would create a chaos that would render the space unsuitable for any form of worship. Founders' Chapel, a safe and secure space for the Ministry of Contemplation, continues in its role as a focus for the devotions of an evangelical community, a community which it serves perfectly well, demonstrating that a church founded on any one of the Six Plans can embrace all the ministries of the Christian church as set out in the Cycle of Worship.

The First Plan

## Bloordale United Church, Toronto.
John Layng, Architect. 1965

A simple suburban church that puts the Eucharist at the center. The communion table has a central location which gives a constant reminder of the sacraments and the faith. Here there is no wish to make a bold statement about the centrality of the faith. Rather, this church has been content to provide its parishioners with humble service, year after year.

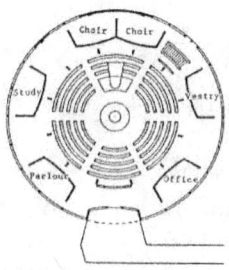

FIGURE 43. The plan of Bloordale United Church in Toronto. A ring of laminated wood arches creates both the structure and the space.

There are many ancient models for this form of worship. Among the traditions of Native People of the North American Continent, when there is a decision to be made a community seats itself in a circle. Each participant in turn may speak while holding the Talking Stick, which is then passed to the next person. The space in the center of the circle is left empty: this is the space for the Great Spirit.

FIGURE 44. The Communion Table is in the center at Bloordale United Church.

At Bloordale United Church the form of worship reflects community in a similar way. Readings and proclamations of the Word are not directed to every individual present as is the case in a lecture hall or auditorium, Rather, the Word is offered into the space at the center of the community, where the community as a whole can receive it.

The First Plan

## The Metropolitan Cathedral of Christ the King, Liverpool
Sir Frederick Gibberd, Architect. 1959

The Cathedral of Christ the King demonstrates how Sacred Inwardness can be achieved for a gathering of two thousand worshipers. The previous examples of Sacred Inwardness share a quality of intimacy, but for a very large gathering the First Plan comes into its own. No other plan can accommodate such a large gathering of worshipers so close to the altar.

The Catholic Diocese of Liverpool was established in 1850, and in 1928 work started on its cathedral. Sir Edwin Lutyens, one of the great architects of the day, designed for the site a vast Romanesque pile. He and the Archbishop were prepared to wait for four hundred years for its completion. However, ten years later, when construction had just got out of the ground it became obvious that building costs were rising faster than the building was rising. It was time for an agonizing reappraisal. The Lutyens basement crypt was roofed over, and things stayed on hold for the next twenty years.

Then in 1959 an architectural competition was announced for the completion of the Cathedral. It was decided to retain the crypt, because it had cost so much already, so the competition was about topping off the crypt with a more cost-effective superstructure. Frederick Gibberd (later Sir Frederick) won the competition with a proposal to extend the roof of the Lutyens crypt as a terrace and on this to build the conical structure we see today, affectionately known as Paddy's wigwam. This structure has a central altar under a huge stained glass lantern, and a perimeter formed by a ring of chapels and oratories. The exterior of the Cathedral is illustrated as the Chapel of Contemplation in Figure 19, page 37.

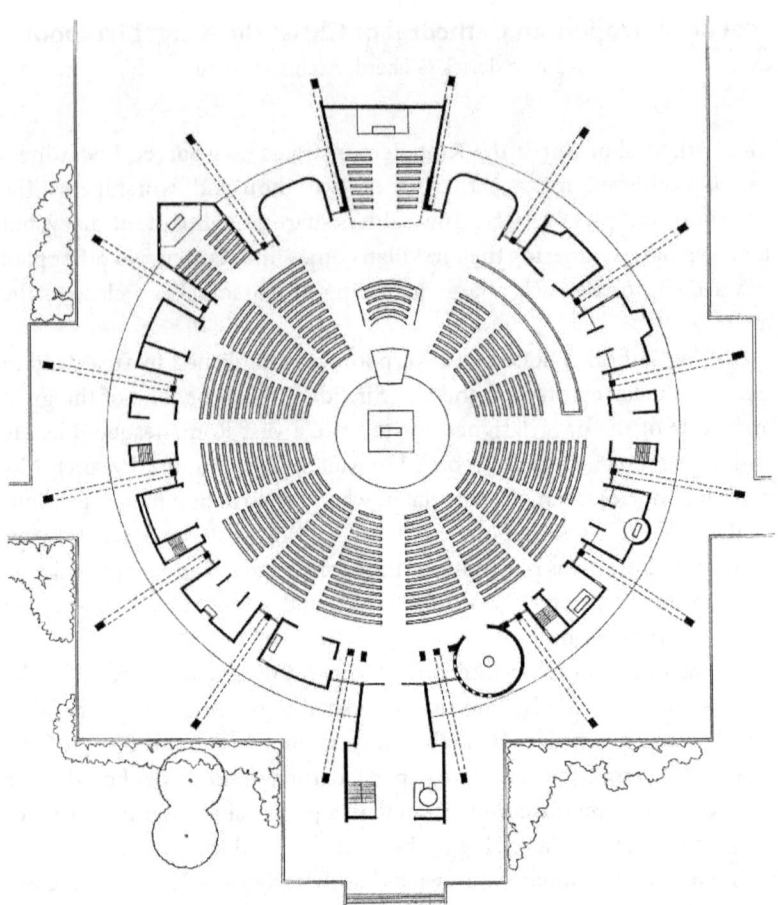

FIGURE 45. Plan of the Metropolitan Cathedral of Christ the King in Liverpool. The conical structure is set on a raised plaza. Part of the plaza forms a roof to the original crypt of the cathedral, all that we have of the original Lutyens design.

THE FIRST PLAN

FIGURE 46. The centralized plan can also work for very large gatherings. Two thousand worship in Liverpool Cathedral.

In Liverpool Cathedral Sacred Inwardness is exemplified first in the circular seating plan, where worshipers focus on a central altar. This is reinforced by the solidity of the walls in creating inner peace. Contact with the outside is minimized. Entrances are downplayed to the point where they are hard to find. There are few windows, and those are filled with a dense stained glass so the outside cannot be seen. Thus we have an inward-looking space for an inward-looking congregation, safe from any conflict outside. This is particularly valuable in Liverpool, a city that had been called "The Capital of Ireland" on account of its vast Irish population, and which has at times suffered from the same sectarian violence as has afflicted Belfast. So these strong walls preserve an inner peace and fulfill the spiritual purpose of the First Plan.

# Chapter 6: The Second Plan *for* the Ministry of Pastoral Care

**Sacred Meeting**

*The people remember the world.*

*By entering the sanctuary
the people have separated themselves from the world
but they are the same people that have been shaped by the world.*

*The people seek peace while remembering conflict.
They seek healing, while remembering pain.
They seek faith, while remembering fear.*

*The Second Plan accepts this duality:
the duality of the Perfection of Christ,
and the cares, afflictions, and fears of the people:
the people coming together in sacred meeting.*

The duality is expressed by forming the walls in the shape of two circular arcs, or two intersecting domes. The smaller dome surrounds the altar. The candles on the altar illuminate it, brilliantly. The walls of this chalice are strong, without openings. They withstand the wuorld and preserve a heavenly peace. In this peace the people gather together in the larger dome. the lights of the a The walls of this dome do not have to be so strong. They do not have to withstand the world. The people are not afraid of the world, or rather, they have the courage to bring their worldly fears with them when they come to worship. They gather as whole persons with all their humanity, their sexuality, their creativity. Light from the chalice spills out over them, a light not from the world but from the Holy Spirit.

# THE SECOND PLAN

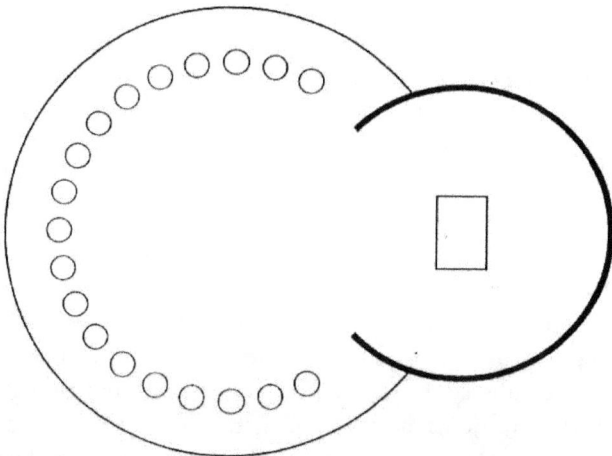

FIGURE 47. The Second Plan: Sacred Meeting, for the ministry of Pastoral Care.

The essential features of the Second Plan are: strong walls to preserve the safety of the space; permeable walls to allow the people to enter; and most importantly free and unimpeded access between the People and the Sacraments.

The point where the two domes meet is the place where the space is the most restricted and the energy is highest. Many churches have a chancel arch at this point where the two spaces meet. In medieval churches there would often be a rood screen of wooden arches at this point supporting a carved wooden cross ("rood" is the Old English word for cross) to further indicate the dual nature of the two spaces.

The people, unworthy but entitled, stand a little way off. They look towards the Chalice. They respond to the bidding "Come unto me, all you that are heavy laden". They approach the altar. There are no barriers. Access is easy. Any barrier here would be a blasphemy. The necessary characteristics of the Second Plan, as listed on page 4, are exterior walls which are both permeable and strong to allow easy entry while keeping the interior safe, and, most importantly, for the People to have free and unimpeded access to the Sacrament.

Christ understands the wounds of the people as He was wounded. He understands hunger, rejection, betrayal, and invites his people to the feast. The light from the altar shines out over all those gathered in Sacred

Meeting. Here forgiveness, redemption and healing are possibilities. The Second Plan is a model of Heaven and Earth.

In rural areas, where community services may be limited, an important function of the church is to offer pastoral care to a congregation. This ministry of caring finds its most fluent expression in Sacred Meeting. Consequently it is found that most rural churches are founded on the Second Plan. If we were to visualize in our mind's eye a small church in a typical village the Second Plan would probably be the basis of our imaginings.

In urban areas, in major cities, the Second Plan is appropriate for the worship of those who feel the pressures of the world. The poor, the disenfranchised, the addicted, those in despair, can find strength here. Those on an inner journey, those in therapy, those in care, can find support. Sacred Meeting welcomes all those who are burdened, oppressed, or engaged in an inner struggle. It accepts that the world is sometimes a harsh and cruel place. It is the Plan that supports the ministry of Pastoral Care. Yet ultimately there is a sadness in this Plan. A sadness that while we are healing, others are suffering.

**A History of Duality**

The Second Plan is a dualism that accepts both an imperfect people and a Perfect Christ. This has caused problems throughout the centuries. As soon as the church acquired power and property the priesthood became an elite. To sustain this they felt they had to separate themselves from the people, which created a new dualism between an imperfect people and a perfect and infallible priesthood. This was expressed by moving the altar and its retinue of priests to a high and distant place.

In the sixteenth century Bishop Hooper of Gloucester was afraid that people might worship the altar and fall into the sin of idolatry[35]. To defend against this he advocated that the altar be moved into a separate room where the public could not see it.

In the seventeenth century William Laud, Archbishop of Canterbury, was afraid that a central altar in the midst of the people might not be respected by the people. He directed that the altar should be set against the east wall of the church, where it could be made more

---

34. Hooper, A Holy Confession, 52.

impressive with screens, drapes, canopies and decorations. It is interesting that both these gentlemen advocated moving the altar away from the people, but for opposite reasons. Laud's legacy is with us today, his innovation we now regard as the norm, albeit a changing one.

The Second Plan cannot countenance these barriers between a people and a sacrament. It exists to overcome barriers. It expresses a coming together so those who feel a separation can enter and be made whole. The light shines equally on everybody; it does not shine brighter on an elite few. The purpose of Sacred Meeting is to illuminate the people, not to dominate or dazzle them. We must be careful. The Second Plan is a form of a worshiping people, not the form of building. There are many buildings that express duality and most of them are not exemplars of Sacred Meeting. The test is that the demarcation between the two spaces does not impede the light, and the people have equal, free and direct access to it. Historic arrangements that create an elite class of people are not consistent with the Second Plan. In so many churches it is a disturbing mockery that many who enter feeling unworthy also leave feeling unworthy. Forgive us.

> *For those who arrive hungry and are sent hungry away,*
> *forgive us.*

> *For those who are kept at a distance,*
> *forgive us.*

> *For those who keep the light for themselves,*
> *forgive us.*

> *For offences committed in Your Name,*
> *have mercy on us.*

Rebuilding the Church

## Holy Trinity Ukrainian Greek-Orthodox Metropolitan Cathedral, Winnipeg
Green, Blankstein, Russell, Architects. 1974.

The dualism of the Second Plan reaches an extreme in the Eastern Communions. The altar and the people are separated by a dividing screen, the iconostasis. The altar is in effect banished to another room, out of sight of the worshipers. It is not part of the worship space.

For a long time I had known that congregational involvement in worship is a self-evident good, so it was with some trepidation I accepted an invitation to attend a Greek Orthodox service for Pentecost. This experience was even more disturbing than I had anticipated: to my consternation I found I had to abandon some deeply held prejudices. Certainly there was a priestly elite. Magnificently crowned and costumed popes with flowing robes and flowing beards processed through the church, entered a doorway in the iconostasis, and closed the door. Here they performed rituals known only to themselves, while we the people just stood around and let them do whatever they needed to do. Occasionally one of them would come to the doorway and give us an update on the proceedings. Communication also took place over the screen: at the point in the service when the priest was censing the altar one of the altar-boys operated a clockwork mechanism which caused a carved and gilded dove impaled on a threaded rod to rise shakily above the iconostasis. Apart from these signs and portents what they were doing behind the screen was a mystery. I remember the comfort of that; the feeling of security that worship was being looked after by experts. They had the training, the knowledge, the skill and the equipment to do what needed to be done. It was like a visitation from the computer repair man, servicing the hardware with nine sorts of screwdrivers. Trusting them completely I was relieved of all anxiety about language, liturgy, and process.

At one point in the proceedings some members of the congregation who had fasted up to that point went up to the front to receive communion. The priest brought out a cup of croutons floating in wine. He served a small portion to each communicant with a tiny spoon, invoking memories of early childhood. For the rest of us baskets of blessed bread were stacked up at the door, and as we left we took some home with us for the following morning's breakfast. Light from the

# The Second Plan

Chalice flooded all over us, and we did not have to do anything to deserve it. We were blessed, as of right.

As an example I have selected Holy Trinity Ukrainian Greek-Orthodox Metropolitan Cathedral in Winnipeg, which stands as a monument[36] to "The Canadian-Ukrainian pioneer who answered the call of a new land, far from his oppressed homeland, and who has so diligently guarded the spiritual gifts of his faith and his culture for the benefit of his children and the enrichment of Canada."

This unusual church represents an attempt at an impossible compromise between asceticism and exuberance. The church was modeled on an ancient church in Kiev, the architects were modeled on Mies van der Rohe. The original church was covered with decoration, every square inch of which told a story, and from which "... even those who cannot read may learn the history of Christ's Church and doctrine. It has been said that the Orthodox Church has two Gospels, one written and one visual. Icons are considered to belong not to the realm of art but to that of theology. They are visual sermons. Just as Christ used his physical body to communicate with man, so the Orthodox Church today continues to use the material world (wood, metal, paint, etc.) to make God known to man."

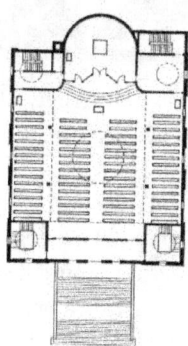

FIGURE 48, Plan of the Holy Trinity Metropolitan Ukrainian Greek-Orthodox Cathedral, Winnipeg. The exterior is illustrated in Figure 19, page 37.

35. Rauliuk, *A Welcome*, 2.

This presented real problems to the architects, who had been, up to that point, the leading exponents in the Canadian prairies of the minimalist stripped-down International Style—St. Gregory the Illuminator meets St. James the Less.

FIGURE 49. The iconostasis of the Holy Trinity Metropolitan Ukrainian Greek-Orthodox Cathedral. In the struggle between plain and fancy, fancy wins.

How could they cope with this decorative imperative? Would they be tempted to abandon their path of austere purity and indulge in all manner of chromatic enthusiasm? Would it set a precedent—influencing the rest of their work? Might it create a brand-new Prairies Style

The solution the architects adopted was one of containment: to restrict all this dangerous decoration to the iconostasis. By doing this they hoped they would be creating a plain interior in which the decorated iconostasis could be contained safely as a "design feature". However it did not work out in that way. The decoration has such overpowering energy and integrity it dominates the space and carries everything along with it, creating a highly decorative interior, but one with some curiously plain walls.

## The Second Plan

The seating embodies another compromise. Traditionally, in a orthodox church, there is no seating for the congregation—everybody stands. This frees the congregation to move around during the service, responding to the various promptings of the liturgy and adding an extra dimension to worship.

The most important feature of Sacred Meeting is the access of the People to the Sacrament. At first sight it might appear that the iconostasis sets up a barrier between the people and the sacraments. However when we refer to the archetypal plan for this ministry (figure 47) we see that the walls are to be both permeable and solid. The permeable walls allow free access to the space; the solid walls are protective to keep the space safe from outside forces. For the Eastern Communions the iconostasis provides the protection for the altar. The consecration of the bread takes place "off-site" in a separate room, as did its baking, but it is received by the people in the heart of their worship space, so the People have free and unimpeded access to the Sacrament, which is the essential feature of the Second Plan.

## All Saints Anglican Church, Sherbourne Street, Toronto.
Lionel Yorke, Architect. 1874.

Even on a rainy weekday afternoon in the Fall the church is full. A lunch counter in the corner is serving three sorts of waxed-paper-wrapped sandwiches and coffee at twenty-five cents a cup.

FIGURE 50. Food for the body, food for the soul, both available at All Saints Church, Toronto.

A hum of conversation fills the room while a television with the sound turned down mindlessly projects reruns of "The Days of Our Lives" to nobody in particular. A few desks ranged against the wall are occupied by various social agencies who seem to be permanently on the phone. This is All Saints Anglican Church in Toronto, a church which ministers to the needs of the economically disadvantaged, the homeless, and the transient. It provides space, shelter, and community. Anywhere in North America, from coast to coast, when transient people refer to the Church in Toronto they mean All Saints.

There are hostels and missions in Toronto which will provide a night's lodging, but these put people out at eight in the morning, and often they have no place to go until the following evening. On fine days they can go out into the streets or gather in the parks, but when the weather is bad their only option is to shelter in shopping malls until they are ushered out by private security personnel charged with protecting our economic values. All Saints provides a place for people to be during the day—it is living room, lounge, café, and club to a large and continually changing population.

It was not always like this. In the 1870's All Saints Church was set in a fashionable residential area and on a Thursday afternoon the church would be as empty as all the other churches in the Diocese. But with the expanding city the wealthy moved out. Their imposing mansions were recycled into rooming houses, sometimes euphemistically called hotels, and the area became a home to the poor.

Then in the 1970's there was a second invasion. Urban living had become the new fashion for the upwardly mobile, and the suburban exiles came back into town, buying up and restoring the properties they had previously vacated. Sand was blasted, paint was scraped, "27" became *"Number Twenty-Seven"* in curly script, and cheap housing became expensive. The poor were displaced from their homes, and All Saints became a parish of the homeless and the dispossessed.

The church still has links with its fashionable past. The interior still has some fine nineteenth-century joinery and decorative brickwork. Brass screens and a glittering eagle grace the chancel. There used to be some fine bronze chandeliers but they did not put out much light so they were sold to an antique dealer for five thousand dollars. Some of this money was used to install fluorescent lighting, and the rest went to support the program.

The worshiping community is quite protective of the sanctuary; in fact they have created a sort of iconostasis fashioned out of a pair of space dividers from somebody's office (moved to one side for the purposes of the photograph in Figure 50) cloth covered and with chrome legs, to demarcate the twin spaces of Sacred Meeting. The daytime users are also very respectful of the area set aside for worship. Although few of them are religious they have an innate appreciation for sacred space and some have, over time, become worshipers. For them the ritual, the decoration, the liturgy and the music fulfill a need for order and beauty in lives that are not always orderly and beautiful. In setting out the requirements for a church to serve the poor W. G. Ward[37], one of the founders of the Oxford Movement, wrote:

> "It is necessary to add the very great desirableness of making our services accessible to the poor by all outward emblems and lively ceremonial . . .
>
> "Religious ceremonial, in other cases but an accessory (though a most important one) becomes in these an absolute essential; for in what other way can religious truths be possibly impressed deeply on those whose minds are worn down by unceasing anxiety and care, and whose bodies are exhausted by severe and protracted toil?"

At All Saints Church satisfaction for spiritual needs is as available as the sandwiches.

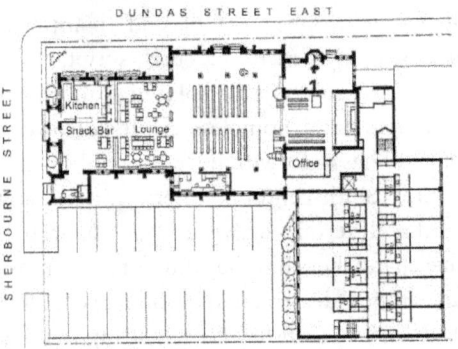

FIGURE 51. Plan of All Saints Anglican Church, Toronto. The nave is used, at different times, as a community center and for worship. The new six-story residence building is seen at lower right.

The church used to have three hundred people sleeping on the floor at night, but this was discontinued because it was perceived as a band-aid solution which merely perpetuated and condoned an inherently unsatisfactory situation. Instead, the church lobbied for funding, and spear-headed the construction of a six-story residential building adjacent to the church. There are sixty-one suites where single people can live with

---

36. Ward, The Ideal of a Christian Church.

dignity. Some of the residents help with administration, and some have become part of the worshiping community. Here they can have a role of welcoming into the church some of those who have been wounded by the world.

Rebuilding the Church

## Chapel in the Cardinal Flahiff Basilian Centre, Toronto.
Ernest Cormier, Architect. 1931.

Ernest Cormier (1885–1980) was Canada's first great architect, noted mainly for his public buildings. His works include the Supreme Court in Ottawa (1938) and the campus of the University of Montreal. His Art-Deco house on avenue des Pins in Montreal (1930) later became the residence of former Prime Minister Pierre Elliot Trudeau. In 1950 Cormier designed this jewel of a chapel for the Basilian Fathers.

For the chapel to be an exemplar of the Second Plan the walls are required to be strong and protective and at the same time to offer easy access. The strength is obvious—the walls are faced with stone, and although there are windows these are set so high in the walls nobody can look in from outside, and they are glazed with an Art-Deco composition of milky glass with brightly colored accents.

Access needs a bit more explanation. The chapel is attached to the Cardinal Flahiff Basilian Center, a three-story residence for retired priests. Each floor connects with the chapel, which is set on the axis of the main entrance, as seen on the plan illustrated in Figure 52. Access is direct, particularly when compared with the meandering entry route of the Wycliffe Chapel illustrated in Figure 41. The corridor on the second floor of the residence building connects with the choir loft located over the narthex. The third floor of the residence, an infirmary for those older fathers who require nursing care, has a smaller balcony which overlooks the chapel and can be seen at a high level in the photograph of the interior of the chapel in Figure 53. By opening the doors to the balcony the sound of the Mass being sung can be heard by the residents of the nursing floor, so secure access to the space is achieved on many levels.

The most important requirement for the Second Plan is that there should be no impediment or barrier between the People and the Sacrament. The altar is set in the center of the space, just as it was in the examples of the previous chapter where Sacred Inwardness supported the ministry of contemplation, but the feel of the space in the Basilian chapel is quite different. Compared with the Founders' Chapel illustrated in Figure 42, this chapel has much more light and open-ness, and we are much more aware of the presence of other members of the community. Some of the community are seated a mere six feet from the altar, and this physical closeness symbolizes for us the spiritual closeness we all experience.

So far, we have studied examples of the first and second Plans as codified by Rudolf Schwarz. Both Plans embody the parameters People and Sacrament, but in opposite directions. In the First Plan the structure is People-to-Sacrament: the community focuses on the altar. In the Second Plan the structure is Sacrament-to-People: the altar extends its

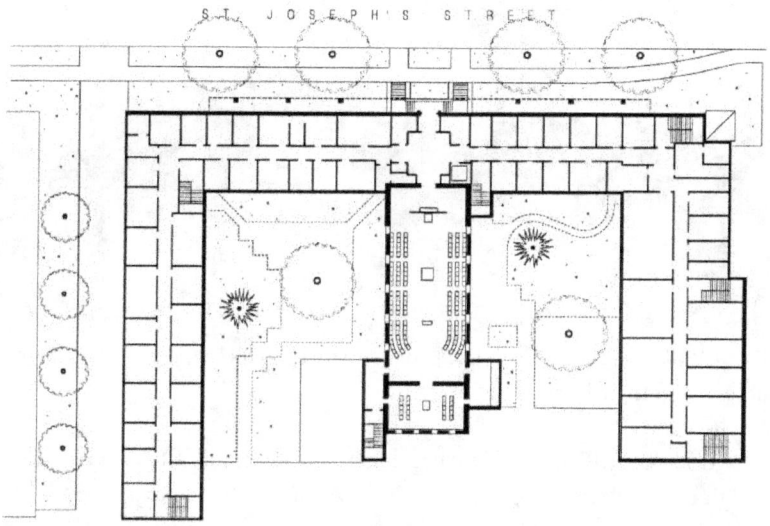

FIGURE 52. Main floor plan of the Cardinal Flahiff Basilian Center showing how the acces to this chapel is much more straightforward than the access to the Wycliffe Chapel as seen in Figure 41.

beneficence over the community. These two Plans embrace the two relationships that are possible between a People and a Sacrament: a human/divine encounter, and these are the relationships that can be expressed in those ministries that offer worship services.
However, for Christians, the world has a unique importance. Christians are required to embrace a duty to the World. That is an essential component of Christian ministry. This worship must find expression in "works" as well as in keeping the faith. Jesus did not spend his time on earth worshiping with his disciples: he sent them out into the world.

FIGURE 53. The Art-Deco interior of St. Basil's Chapel with a central altar is accessed on three levels.

David Jenkins, Bishop of Durham, has said that of all the other-worldly religions Christianity is the most "this-worldly". This is expressed in the remaining four of the Six Plans (to be studied in the next four chapters) all of which have "World" as one of their parameters, enabling a congregation to enrich its ministry by extending its worship to embrace the world around it.

# Chapter 7: The Third Plan *for* the Ministry of Witness

**The Shining**

*The dome is breached.*
*The light shines out into the world.*
*The People and Christ are together.*
*They look out into a world created by God's will,*
*and shaped by man's will.*

*Inside: the people see out into the world.*
*Outside: the world sees the light of the people at prayer.*

*The Third Plan is the Plan of Witness,*
*the plan that proclaims Christ's presence in God's world.*

The dome is pierced and the people see the world. The world into which they were born, the world where they work, the world which is their

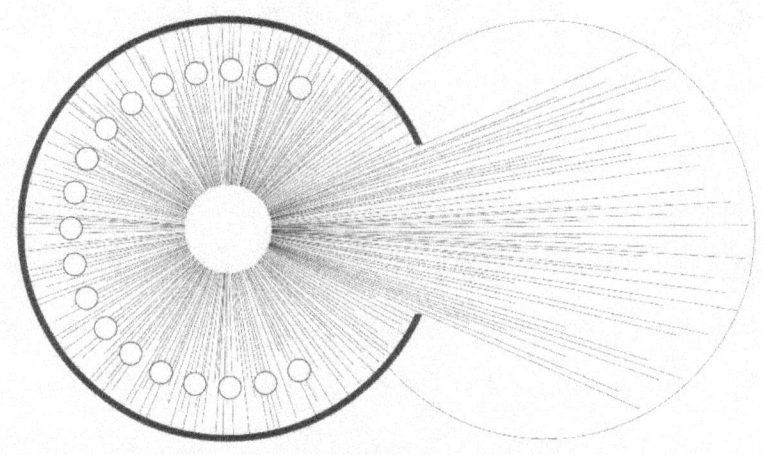

FIGURE 54. The Third Plan: The Shining, for the ministry of Witness.

home. They see the poverty, the greed, the beauty, the crime, the hope. They see the world but they do not go out into the world. The Shining forms a link between the intimacy of the Eucharist and the objectivity of the world outside. This is the bond that holds creation together. The people gather around the altar. The light of the altar shines over the people and out into the world.

The faint circle on the right represents the world. It states that the light of the sacraments is targeted to the world—it is not an aimless emanation. The world sees the light and the world sees the people at prayer. The people at prayer and the light of the Eucharist are the witness of Christ's presence in the world. The Third Plan is the Plan of Witness.

The Third Plan

## St. Peter's Lutheran Church, New York City.

Hugh Stubbins and Associates, Architects. 1976.

St. Peter's Church on Lexington Avenue at 54th Street in downtown Manhattan presents with great clarity an example of the working out of the Third Plan. The archetypal Third Plan is a breached dome. The dome was selected as a way of symbolizing the impenetrable quality of the walls. This does not mean that the building has to be shaped like a dome: rather, it is a way of saying that for the Third Plan the space inside must be secure. In St. Peter's the sanctuary is underground, and this gives us strong walls and a safe space.

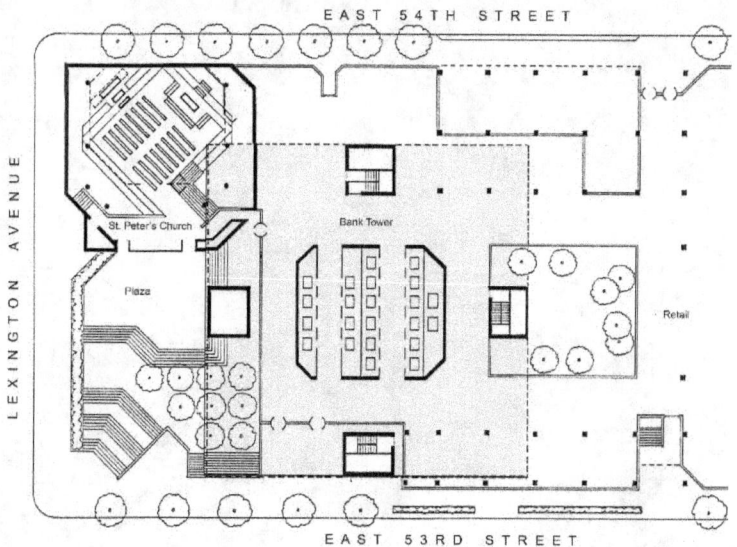

FIGURE 55. Plan of Citicorp Center, Lexington Avenue, New York City. The new St. Peter's Lutheran Church is located at the corner of Lexington and East 54th Street, partially under the overhang of the Citibank office tower. A sunken plaza which gives access to the church connects with the subway station.

The breach in the dome, The Shining, is a way for the worshiping people to see the world, and a way for the light of the Eucharist to be witnessed by the world. In St. Peter's the dome is breached by a tall window over the altar. Through this window can be seen the office towers across the street on Lexington Avenue. Thus the worshipers can see, in the same glance, the altar where they worship and the offices where they work. World and worship are brought together.

Norman McGrath Photographer

FIGURE 56. Work and worship are seen together in St. Peter's Lutheran Church. Everything is movable except the organ and the font.

# The Third Plan

The mission of the Third Plan is Witness. This mission was one of the forces that drove the planning of St. Peter's. There had been a St. Peter's Church at the corner of Lexington and 54th Street since 1862. The original neo-Gothic pile could seat hundreds, but the land it had been sitting on became worth millions. In 1968 the land was sold to the First National City Bank, but with the proviso that a new church would be incorporated into the development. In a letter to the President of Citibank the architect, Hugh Stubbins, wrote:

> "With the church as catalyst and the bank as supporter we can design a new kind of place which all sorts of people will want to enter and become part of. While the church must have its own identity I like to think how it could be enhanced and magnified if we combine it with a new kind of office building. I think, furthermore, that we should be able to see into the church from outside, to see what is going on, be attracted, and become part of it. There is a spirit stirring at Saint Peter's Church that could become a bright light in Manhattan."

Seldom has the mission of Witness been better described. The development that resulted consists of a fifty-nine story office tower, and nestling under the northwest corner of the tower, the new St. Peter's Church. The floor level of the church is at basement level but a lantern in the roof of the church projects through to the sidewalk. Windows in this lantern look down into the church beneath, so the casual passer-by on Lexington Avenue might be surprised to see below him a congregation at prayer. The photograph (fig. 56.) shows that the congregation can also witness the outside world. Through the breach in the dome, the lantern, one can just see the passing Lexington Avenue bus. The passer-by might also see a concert, a lecture, a jazz festival, a folk mass. or just a quiet place to be. The space inside the church accommodates all of these. It is totally flexible: everything in it, with the exception of the font and the organ, is movable. Pews and platforms, altars and lecterns, all can be moved around and stashed away, This means the church can accommodate all sorts of programs. It can be the scene of round-the-clock activity, a perpetual witness. The public has responded to this with enthusiasm. St. Peter's Lutheran Church in Citicorp Center must be considered one of America's most successful urban churches.

REBUILDING THE CHURCH

## St. Thomas's Anglican Church, St. Catharines, Ontario.
Gerald Robinson, Architect and Liturgical Consultant. 1989.

This example shows how a congregation can adapt an existing structure to better suit its needs.

FIGURE 57. The dome is breached. In the front wall of St. Thomas's Anglican Church a large circular arch was constructed. This opening, fitted with glass doors, allows witness to the worship within.

# The Third Plan

There is no doubt that the mission of the congregation of St. Thomas' Church is Witness. Some of their church services are broadcast on local radio and on the Buffalo television station. The church hosts an ambitious program of concerts and musical performances: their choir is noted for its artistry. During the week, the church is full of small children—they have the biggest day-care center in the Niagara Peninsula. It was bizarre that for a congregation so extroverted, so community-minded, their church building should seal them off from the world. Their worship takes place in a stone box.

The original church was designed by William Beebee of Buffalo in 1877, in a style known as Richardson-Romanesque. Its four-square plan, massive walls, and heavy masonry are reminiscent of H. H. Richardson's Trinity Church at Copley Square in Boston. From the outside the church was a fortress. Small windows admitted little daylight—they would be more functional for repelling invaders. The entrance facing the tower was up a massive flight of stone steps, at the top of which one was confronted by heavy oak doors, which looked like they never had been opened in the last fifty years. They offered an access that was impossible for the handicapped and threatening for everybody else. The building conveyed the message that its purpose was to defend itself against the onslaughts of an enemy, not to welcome the People of God.

The congregation were surprised when I showed them the image that they were projecting to the world; an image totally at odds with the ministry of Witness. They embarked on a lengthy process of self-examination, and decided to undertake a program of renovation and renewal. The changes they agreed on were:

> 1. To make the building accessible to everybody by raising the level of the ground at the front so people could walk straight in, eliminating the steps.
>
> 2. To make the building more welcoming, by cutting a large arched opening into the front wall of the church, an opening fitted with an all-glass entrance. Thus the Church would be open to the City, and the City to the Church.
>
> 3. To replace the pews by chairs to allow for a central altar, and to enable worship to be more flexible.

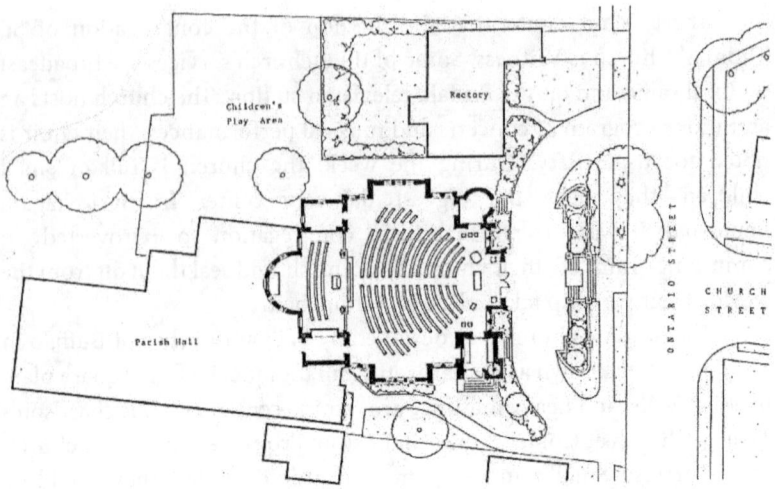

FIGURE 58. Plan of St. Thomas', showing the arrangement of seating for the Service of Dedication. Temporarily the movable altar was set just inside the glass doors, enabling the congregation to face both the Sacrament and the City.

The resulting arrangement, as illustrated in Figure 59, created what has been called[38] "the finest liturgical space in North America". A central altar creates a natural focus for the devotions of the community, a drawing-together of the People and the Sacrament into the intimacy associated with Pastoral Care, and it is the energy generated by that worship that shines out into the world and fulfills the ministry of Witness.

After the renovations the flexibility of the seating was used for a service of dedication, the layout for which is illustrated in Figure 58. The altar was set just inside the glass doors at the back of the church, and the chairs were turned to face the altar in this position. The people saw the traditional ceremony of Bishop Bothwell arriving at the entrance, banging at the glass doors (gently) with his crozier, and requesting admission. For the first time the people could see, in the same view, the Sacrament and the City of St. Catharines.

They saw even more than they had anticipated: during the service some teenagers in a black Mustang roared up the ramp, got out, and

---

37. Bishop Joachim Fricker at the 1992 Trinity Divinity Associates Conference.

peered in through the glass doors. When they held their faces close to the glass the new arrivals were surprised to see several hundred people looking back at them. This new interest in the Anglican Church by the city's youth was considered a good omen for future ministry.

FIGURE 59. An interior view of the new glass-filled archway by which the congregation can see the City and the world can witness a people at prayer. Flexible seating and a movable altar permit many different liturgical arrangements within a very traditional Romanesque space.

The congregation has truly experienced the opening of the dome, and their Shining is the touchstone for the ministry of Witness.

## Church of the Good Shepherd, Lake Tepako, New Zealand.
### R. D. S. Harman, Architect. 1935.

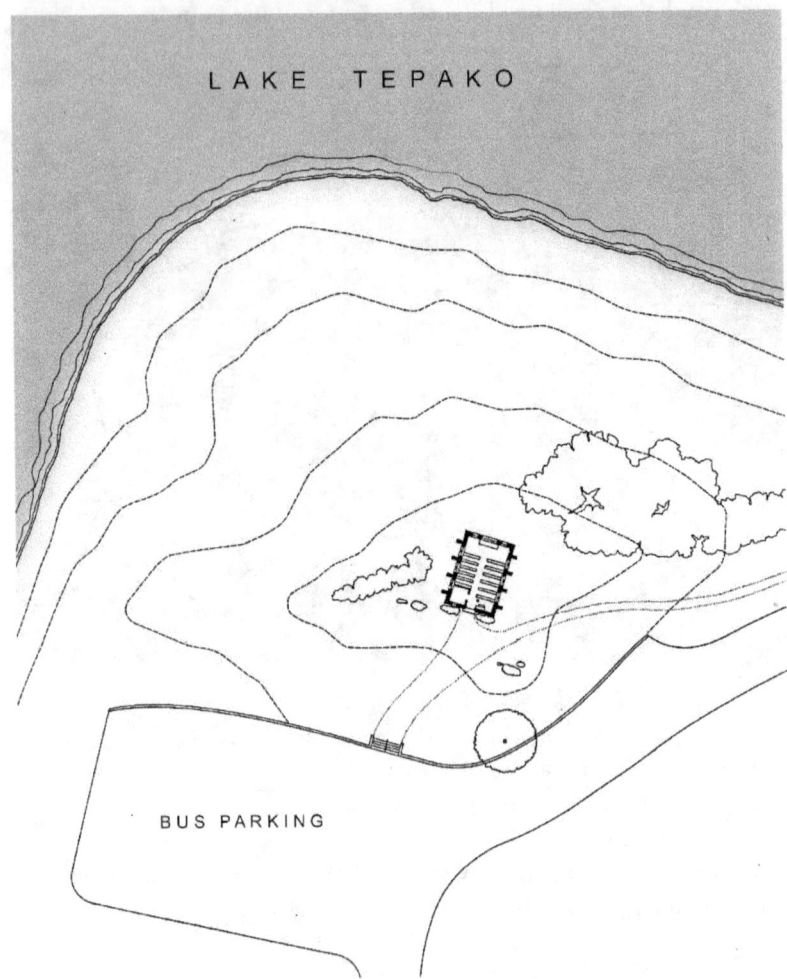

FIGURE 62. The Church of the Good Shepherd, on a rise overlooking Lake Tepako a New Zealand beauty spot.

FIGURE 60. Witness at the rest stop: beautiful Lake Tepako, with its snow-capped mountains . . .

FIGURE 61. . . . visible from within the Church of the Good Shepherd.

A small wayside chapel, set in an area of breathtaking beauty. Every day twelve tour buses discharge their passengers at this point for a twenty-minute rest stop; and there is the chapel waiting in silent witness.

Inside, the wayfarers are welcomed into an interior of quiet and contemplation. The noise of the diesels is stilled. Behind the altar a window reveals some of the wonders of God's Creation

We cannot stay long. We have a schedule to keep. But we can witness, in the shining landscape, the shining of the spirit.

# The Third Plan

The Temple of the Children of Peace, Sharon, Ontario.
Ebenezer Doan, Builder, 1831.

In 1800, twenty Quaker families from Vermont emigrated to Upper Canada to establish a settlement north of Toronto. By 1806 the community had grown to a hundred families. The new meeting was not long established when a series of crises disrupted the expected harmony among "Friends"[39], and a group of dissidents, led by David Willson, split off from the Quakers. They established themselves at nearby Sharon, calling themselves the Children of Peace.

Their theological differences hinged around whether Christ was Man and his spirit is God, or God and His spirit was made flesh. This dispute surfaced at a time when the War of 1812 was introducing other stresses into the community, and some twenty families took the opportunity to split off from the parent body.

The Children built a series of meeting houses, quite different in style from those of their Quaker forebears. David Willson was a carpenter by trade. In his autobiography[40] he writes:

> "I inclined to mechanical business in joining timber one part to another, by which I have erected in the village of Sharon memorials of the pattern the Lord hath given for the erection of his House. And with the pen have I drawn the lines of his spirit as to me they have been given. I commit them to memory as a debt I owe to the Lord which I am unable to pay; nevertheless, I trust they will remain to be the mark of a good design."

---

38. Schrauwers. The Politics of Schism.

39. Willson. A Collection of Items.

FIGURE 63. On a country road in southern Ontario, the extraordinary Sharon Temple.

FIGURE 64. The Temple is even more extraordinary by night during the Illuminations

# The Third Plan

This inspiration resulted in a flamboyant design, stepped in tiers like a wedding cake, with tiny square turrets in each corner. The central lantern is supported by four columns named for the four cardinal virtues. Surrounding these are twelve columns named for the Apostles, which support a music gallery at the second floor, reached by a soaring "Jacob's Ladder". Willson departed from the plain-ness of his Quaker forebears by his instructions to "ornament the Christian church with all the glory of Israel". He also introduced music into worship; the church had a pipe organ, a choir, and a flourishing silver band.

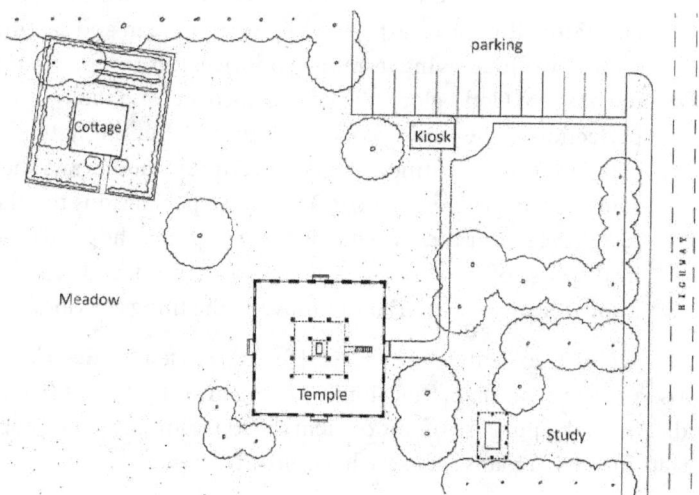

FIGURE 65. Plan of the Temple of the Children of Peace, Sharon, Ontario. The small building between the Temple and the road is David Willson's study where wrote his sermons.

The plan is based on biblical references to Solomon's Temple, to Freemasonry, and to the New Jerusalem. It is a perfect square, because Willson and his followers believed in "dealing squarely" with people. And each wall has an equal number of windows, so that "the light of the gospel" could shine "equally the same on all people", a perfect example of the working of the ministry of Witness. The light was literal as well as metaphorical: a candle sconce was set in every window and turret. The building presented[41] "a very beautiful appearance when lighted, there being 2,952 panes of glass in the windows and spires."

The name "Children of Peace" was carefully chosen. "Children" indicates that the group had no Elders, as did orthodox Quaker societies; and "Peace" represents freedom from doctrinal argument as they had no doctrine except the bible. The group did not practice evangelism, holding this to be a form of coercion. Willson distinguishes between the ministries of witness and evangelism, writing[42]:

> "We have built a house to sacrifice to God, feed the hungry, and clothe the naked. Any stranger may come in and sacrifice with us without giving us money or price. It is for the various purposes of God's glory, the end of doctrine, and the perfection of the world. We are not perfect, but the system adopted by us is justified of God in scripture, and draws the soul near unto God in Christ. We use no persuasions to others to believe in our theory, knowing all things are the Lord's, and he disposes of them according to his own mind; and that the human heart hath no right to move in the things of God."

The builder of the Temple, Ebenezer Doan[43], gracefully describes its purpose as an invocation of The Shining; being in and yet apart from the world: "As for the purpose of our contemplated building, it is to prepare the heart for such a mansion as we have already."

---

40. McArthur, Children of Peace.
41. Willson, A Short Word to Visitors.
42. McArthur, Children of Peace.

## The Forms of Witness

Four churches have been selected as examples of the ministry of witness. They are:

St. Peter's Lutheran, New York

St. Thomas' Anglican Church, St. Catharines, Ontario.

Church of the Good Shepherd, Lake Tekapo, New Zealand, and

The Temple of the Children of Peace, Sharon, Ontario.

These churches are very different from one another. There is no recognizable form or common thread uniting them. Their only commonality is their role, which is symbolized in the beams of light emanating from Schwarz's Third Plan. They are all witnessing to people, but people in very different situations. The four examples selected witness to Christ's presence on the sidewalks of Manhattan, on the main street of a country town, on the shores of a beautiful placid lake, and on a country road. This variety of form reflects the variety of circumstances in which people can find opportunities for witness, so the Third Plan is represented by the most divers building styles. At the same time the built form of the church is more vitally important to the ministry of Witness than it is for any other ministry. That is because for Witness the building itself is the prime instrument of expression. Perhaps some of the awe that we feel when we enter a well-crafted but empty church is because we are witnessing the space itself worshiping; that its clarity, grace, and order are indeed praising the Lord.

## The Virtual Church

Witness is the ministry of many of those churches that proclaim themselves as "evangelical". This term, as a description of a worship style rather than a ministry, embraces such denominations as the Pentecostals, together with such stand-alone churches as Willow Creek. Typically, these churches are styled as auditoriums where thousands are assembled for a technically-sophisticated presentation of a liturgy that borrows heavily from pop culture and easy-listening. Usually the building itself is nondescript—merely an envelope to contain the air-conditioning. In spite of their apparent success a difficulty these churches face is that their gatherings do not foster community, they are just too big - and community is essential for Christian worship. The Fellowship Baptist Church studied the dynamics of relationships in congregations of various sizes and concluded that 350 is the maximum size for a congregation if everybody is going to know a sufficient number of people to have a sense of belonging. Beyond this size a significant number of individuals will feel that they are just passing through, worshiping with strangers, so when a Fellowship Baptist congregation grows to this point it is invited to think about peeling-off a hundred members to plant a new church. A church requires intimacy, the key factor in the ministry of evangelism, and this is so we may love one another.

The evangelical enthusiasm for enrolling the newcomer may become such a dominating thrust the faithful may become ignored. When liturgies are simplified to the point of being instantly accessible to the newcomer they are necessarily superficial. They never reach the point of exploring the depths of religious feeling, consequently they offer little to grow into, few opportunities to learn, and not much of a sense of community. The result is a repetitive feel-good blandness, and few will find it rewarding to repeat these experiences for more than five years.

If there is little sense of community in these vast gatherings there is even less in those virtual churches operated by TV Evangelists. They use vast technical and musical resources to present a version of the Sacraments to the World. These are the parameters of the ministry of Witness, but this ministry is to be in the context of a worshiping community. A studio audience cannot be considered to be such a community. It does not bind itself together with bonds of mutual affection, support, care, and vocation. The community which the studio audience attempts to portray might be appealing but it has no reality. It is a virtual image with no substance.

That said, there is much that traditional churches can learn from these evangelical institutions; how to welcome the visitor with the best parking spot, a big smile, an embroidered bookmark or a ball-point pen, familiar music, and a comfortable seat from which everything can be seen and heard. Few traditional churches do this, or even care to, so their shrinking attendance is predictable and deserved. Similarly, evangelicals can learn from the traditional churches the importance of the human need to belong; the need to experience the reality of a place as an image of God's creation, and a need for community with both the present gathering of worshipers and those who have gone before. The challenge for the next century will be to allow these evangelical and traditional channels to merge and flow together in a single stream of living water.

THE THIRD PLAN

# Interlude: The Dome of Darkness

In The Shining a large opening is created in the dome: a window looking out into the world. This permits communication between the worshipers and the world, which is the essential feature of the Third Plan.

Another way to create an opening in the dome would be to make a large skylight in the roof. This is very popular with architects. It offers an easy opportunity to play with light for dramatic effect. This is the quick fix for creating a holy place—such places appearing most holy when they are not cluttered with people. The religious rationale for the skylight is that by admitting light from on high we have created a metaphor for an inflowing of the Holy Spirit—a chimney for Santa Claus.

The drawback of the skylight is that the people cannot see the world. All they can see through the opening is sky.

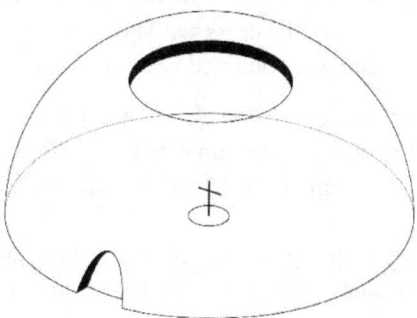

FIGURE 66. The Dome of Darkness: light pours in from above.

This gives rise to another plan, the Dome of Darkness, which is not part of our cycle of plans. It is not part of the cycle because it is not founded on any of the six relationships presented in Figure 18, page 35. In the Dome of Darkness the World is not present: opaque walls keep it at a distance.

For many religions, the World is not a vital component of worship, but for the Christian it is essential. It is the essence of Christianity that God so loved the world that he sent his son to become human like us. So if the world is important to God it must be important to us. It is our embracing of the world that makes the Six Plans possible, and gives Christian architecture its richness.

In the Dome of Darkness there is no World, and there is no community of the People: when we look up to the light we do not see one another. So the Dome of Darkness is built around a private relationship between the Sacrament and an individual. By studying this plan we may learn of the unfortunate results that may ensue when we select, for a church, a plan which is "off the track". This Plan embodies but a single parameter, an isolated Sacrament, so there can be no relationship and therefore no Christian worship.

A dome with a large opening or oculus in the roof is not often used in Christian churches, and when it is used it is usually for mausoleums and baptisteries. For mausoleums it can represent the broken tomb, with light streaming in from above. A similar image can be applied to baptism, which can be represented as a symbolic drowning and rebirth. Cyril of Jerusalem[44] wrote:

> "You were led to the holy pool of divine baptism, as Christ taken down from the cross was laid in the tomb already prepared. You were plunged in the water and rose out of it."

The light streams down into the dome but none escapes, hence the chalice is dark. The people communicate only with the light. They raise their eyes to it in worship. They do not see one another, or anything of the world.

This form of building is used by many Eastern religions. Many temples, some famous ones, are constructed in this way. This form stresses the goal of personal enlightenment, a private path. It is a matter of indifference to the enlightened that, outside, thousands are routinely dying in the street.

The Dome of Darkness is an appropriate plan for the various fundamentalist assemblies known as the Moral Majority. It expresses the goal of individual, personal salvation. The light streams down vertically from above. The walls of the dome are dark, in contrast to the blinding light from above. Our neighbors are dark. The world is a dark place, sinful and dangerous, full of perfumed temptations and beckoning motels. The people too are dark and in shadow, except for the minority that are standing in the light with us. And as the light grows ever brighter it may reveal darkness even in those closest to us. There is no one that

---

43. Cyril of Jerusalem, *Mystagogical Catechesis*, II: 4.

## The Third Plan

can be trusted completely. The light can see everything. It is as brilliant as the studio lights shining down on TV Evangelists. It is as penetrating as the flash bulbs of the press, always waiting to expose our fall from grace—a fall for which there is no forgiveness, because once we enter or stumble into the dark we are totally cut off from the light. The Dome of Darkness receives light, but what it contains is darkness.

Unfortunately the plan for the Dome of Darkness is quite common because it gives architects a chance to play God. By placing a skylight over the altar they seek a dramatic effect, even though the drama is usually inappropriate and the light from a moving sun usually misses its target. Architects find it hard to resist such temptations, but these you must absolutely forbid. And if you inherit a church which does have a skylight just get some black paint and climb up on to the roof to cover it, as was done by the Toronto Airport Christian Fellowship in their new facility in order to achieve a worship space free of distractions.

The prime example of a space configured on this plan would be the Pantheon in Rome: a pagan temple built by the Emperor Hadrian. It is spanned by a 142-foot dome with a 30-foot opening at the center, which permits rain, and sometimes snow, to fall into the interior. In 609 Pope Boniface IV consecrated the space as a Christian church. The spooky quality of the space led the author[45] of the Da Vinci Code to include it as a venue of psychic significance in his romance, asserting that: "The sixth-century Venerable Bede once wrote that the hole in the Pantheon's roof had been bored by demons trying to escape the building when it was consecrated by Pope Boniface IV."

Other references to such evil presences include a narrative from an occult work[46]:

> "The garland of the trumpet was set afire, and then I saw the aperture of the dome open and a splendid arrow of fire shoot down through the tube of the trumpet and enter the lifeless body. The aperture then was closed again, and the trumpet too was put away."

And, in a warning from the Talmud (Berakhot 6)

---

44. Brown, Angels and Demons.
45. Andrae, The Chemical Wedding.

"If the eye could see the demons that people the universe, life would be impossible."

Clearly the Pope's exorcism was not entirely successful. His incantations did nothing to transform the space so it would be suitable for Christian worship. The Pantheon remains an exemplar of the Dome of Darkness.

The Third Plan

## St. Andrews United Church, Toronto.
Page and Steele, Architects. 1981.

The situation of this church has many aspects in common with an example from the previous chapter, St. Peter's Lutheran in Manhattan, but the differences are instructive.

For a long time there had been a St. Andrews Church on this site on Bloor Street East in Toronto. This is an area that was once part of the remote outskirts of Toronto, but is now a fashionable midtown shopping district. As land values increased the congregation decreased. The few parishioners that were left found they were sitting on a gold-mine.

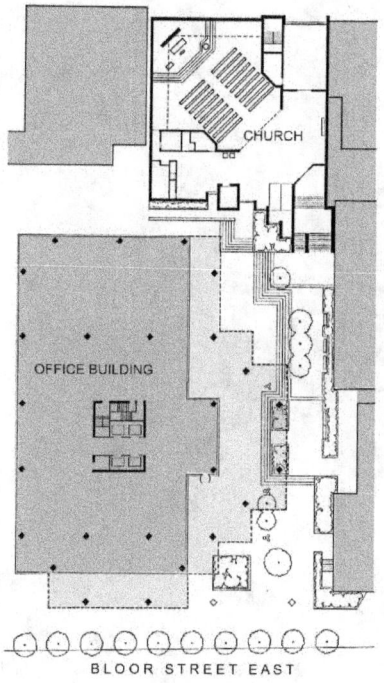

FIGURE 67. Plan of St. Andrews United Church, Toronto.

To exploit this the land was sold to a development corporation as a site for an office building. The huge old church, seating 600, was demolished, and a new smaller church was built on a corner of the site.

So far, this description could apply to either church. The important difference is that the new St. Peter's Church is located right at the corner of Lexington and 54th Street (figure 55) where it stands as a witness to the presence of Christ in the world. On the other hand, St. Andrew's Church in Toronto is located at the back of the site (figure 67), about as far away from the people as it could possibly be.

FIGURE 68. By siting itself as far from the street as possible St. Andrews United Church preserves its privacy.

THE THIRD PLAN

FIGURE 69. Inside, the heavens open for those privileged to climb the Holy Mountain.

This church has been described as "the invisible church"[47]. It is built in a corporate style, with all the stainless steel and reflective glass that term implies. Perhaps it is an advantage for the church to look like an office

46. Sacred Space and Human Needs, Trinity College.

building because anybody seeking a church here would find only a locked door. Inside there is an expression of the theme of the Dome of Darkness. The walls are opaque, the light streams in from above. Our concentration is vertical. A holy mountain of steps and levels thrusts itself up to the light. Atop the mountain is a huge rectangular structure (figure 69), dark and foreboding, rescued from the previous church. It has a most unfortunate resemblance to the monolith in Stanley Kubrick's movie "2001, A Space Odyssey". This dark and towering form dominates the whole space. We shudder at the base of the mountain, overshadowed by the monolith, drenched in the glare from above, and cut off from the world and from one another.

This does not mean that the congregation ignores the world; in fact they provide financial support for many social agencies. Rather, it is to say that by an unhappy combination of circumstances, the space and siting of the building support a form of worship that keeps the world at a distance. This is a lost opportunity. A congregation with a different set of values could have created a small chapel off the elevator lobby of the office building, where thousands of people pass every day. As it is, millions of dollars were expended so a small and privileged congregation could continue to worship at the same address. The Dome of Darkness is the Plan of Privilege. That is what the stones are saying.

I am sure it is not what St. Andrew's congregation wanted. Unwittingly they have sacrificed their own well-being to serve us . . . to serve us by showing us what monsters may be spawned when we stray from the Cycle of Plans.

# Chapter 8: The Fourth Plan *for* the Ministry of Dedication

**Sacred Journey**

*Work needs to be done in the world.*
*The worshipers have found a new security in a common purpose.*
*They no longer need the security provided by the enclosing dome.*
*They are on a march,*
*a pilgrimage,*
*a Sacred Journey.*

*The people have been drawn together by the Eucharist.*
*This gave them strength.*
*Now they are moving into a new place, with new challenges.*

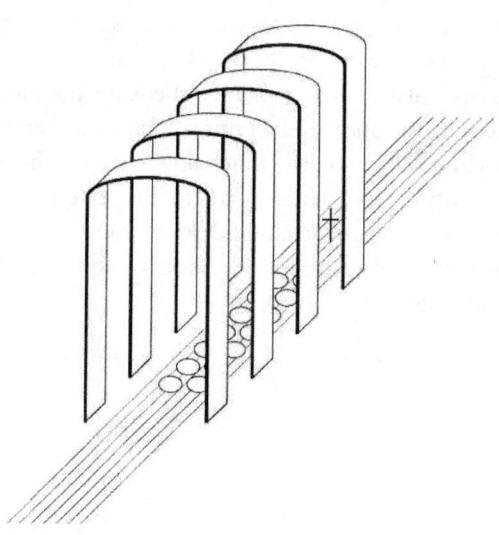

FIGURE 70. The Fourth Plan, Sacred Journey, for the Ministry of Dedication.

The people all face the same direction. They do not need to face one another because they knew they had become a community the moment they committed themselves to their journey. Even though they do not face one another, they are in fact physically close to one another. They are held together by a common faith, and embarked together on a Sacred Journey. Their needs are few. They travel light. Their worship takes place on the road.

The essential features of the Fourth Plan are:

the linear quality of the space, and most importantly,

an endless pathway extending beyond confines of the space.

The Fourth Plan, Sacred Journey, is unlike all the other plans. It has a strong linear quality, to represent Sacred Journey as a passing through time, but the transit does not necessarily have to be expressed by a processional route. In the Church of Sant'Agnese fuori le Mura in Rome (St. Agnes outside the walls) the progression through space is vertical, as in the case of a plant's shoot rising to the light. The foundation of the progression is a tiny chapel in the catacombs, a subterranean shrine to St. Agnes, buried deep in the earth. In the seventh century the site was excavated and the overburden removed to uncover the roof of the chapel, and a handsome basilica was built over it, still mostly underground. This church was the inspiration for Margaret Visser[48] in her book "The Geometry of Love", itself a labor of love. Beneath the altar is a silver sarcophagus bearing the body of the saint, and at an upper level a gallery runs round the church. The gallery, which is at what was the original level of the ground outside, has a doorway to the exterior, offering the metaphor that our lives and livelihood in an outside world, a world which we consider to be so important, is just another incident on an eternal Sacred Journey.

---

47. Visser, The Geometry of Love.

FIGURE 71. Sant'Agnese fuori le Mura in Rome is a vertical expression of the Way, a Journey from a tiny chapel in the catacombs (beneath the floor) to the heavens above.

A subsequent excavation lowered the ground level outside the church to allow for an easier entrance at floor-level, so now the original doorway finds itself high-and-dry half-way up the wall. What has been gained in convenience has been lost as symbolism.

Over the altar, a golden hemi-dome represents a heaven from which an image of the saint looks down on us; and above this dome we know there is yet another celestial dome, traced with the flight paths of angels and 747's.

The Fourth Plan accommodates those who have embarked on a Sacred Journey. It also stands as a representation of that journey. It does not show the place we have started from, that was entirely encompassed in The Shining. It does not show where we shall arrive. That is in the future, not yet available to us. The parallel between life and journey was noted by Gerard Hughes, a Jesuit priest who undertook a pilgrimage from London to Rome in 1978[49]. He observes: "On the road the pilgrim learns that searching for God is already to have found him, and that direction is much more important than destination, because God is not just an end, nor a beginning, but for us he is always a beginning without end."

The ends of the enclosure should be open. The Fourth Plan represents a stop on the Sacred Journey, it is not where the journey stops. We have to be able to see our way ahead. So at the ends of the space there should not be any barriers or heavy decoration that might obstruct or cause us to stumble. The end walls could be glass, so one could see a continuing of the Way, or the ends could be a series of screens, to leave it ambiguous as to where the enclosure ends, so wherever we look, the end is somewhere else. The purpose of Sacred Journey is not a quest to reach God: Sacred Journey is a journey with God. The people carry their altar with them. They have a processional cross, and banners to proclaim their purpose. They worship on the move, knowing they must press on. They know they will not live this minute again.

The Fourth Plan is supportive of those who are brought together for a short time for a common purpose, and who know that later they must separate. It works well for the worship of schools and universities, where the goal is to equip oneself for a life in the world beyond. The ministry of Dedication finds its most extreme expression in monasteries

---

48. Hughes, In Search of a Way.

and closed communities where a separate or private World has been created for the People, a world more perfect, without some of the temptations of the outside world. The Fourth Plan is also supportive of the worship of the business community, those whose labor in the World supports the worship of the People in an act of dedication.

With great wisdom Pope John XXIII[50] spoke of the whole church as " a pilgrim people of God. The church is seen as a Church of Pilgrimage to its true native land." implying that we should not overly burden ourselves with institutions and traditions, but rejoice in the freedom of the faith. Just as this faith has the power to continually restore and renew us, so must the church ever and always renew itself. We cannot rest on our laurels. "The catholic church is summoned to a continual reformation, she is the Church on her Pilgrim Way."[51] We all have something to learn from Sacred Journey, because it is Sacred Journey that continually confronts us with something new. The Fourth Plan is the plan of Dedication.

Many churches, perhaps most churches, have the seating arranged to allow for a central aisle, but few of these churches are exemplars of the Fourth Plan. An essential feature of Sacred Journey is an expression that the entire congregation is on the move. This is not what we experience when we witness a liturgical procession moving down an aisle which bisects a static congregation. Regarding processions, in the 1907 "The Parson's Handbook" Percy Dearmer[52] wrote:

> "The procession is a distinct, significant act of worship: it is not an aimless walk round the church; but it has a definite object, such as the Rood, the Lord's Table, or the Font.
>
> "A procession is not the triumphant entry and exit of the choir, nor is any such thing known to the Church as a 'recessional'.
>
> "Properly, the choir should go quietly to their places when they arrive, and occupy the time before the service with prayer and recollectedness in the stalls, instead of chatting in the vestry.

---

49. Reid, Vatican II, 20

50. Reid, Vatican II, 42

51. Dearmer, Parson's Handbook.

If, however, they go in all together in processional order, no hymn should be sung, nor should there be any special hymn to accompany their return; and above all, no cross should be carried. They should be well settled in their places before the ministers enter.

"The Prayer Book orders three processions:

(1) The procession to the altar in the Marriage Service.

(2) The procession at a funeral.

(3) The procession to the font at Holy Baptism.

"These are all true processions, full of significance and solemnity: the first is the solemn conducting of the married pair to the altar, there to be blessed; the second is the solemn carrying up of the corpse to receive the last offices of the church; the third is the going forth of the priest and his assistants to meet the infant at the font and receive it into the Church."

These processions are purposeful, and are to achieve a definite destination, while a pilgrimage has the journey itself as its goal. In the one case it is usual to see an elite entourage moving through a static assembly of observers, in the other all the worshipers are on the move.

**Medieval Space**

Some beautiful cathedrals have been built on the principle of Sacred Journey, not always intentionally. In the Middle Ages available technology limited distances which roofs could span. Buildings could not be made very wide. If it was desired to make a very large space the only way to do it was to make it of moderate width, and very long. Thus many cathedrals were obliged to represent Sacred Journey, because such modern techniques as the shell dome and the space frame were not available to them. It is interesting to note that even though we are now free of these constraints we still sometimes submit to them. Many believe that this is what a "real" church should look like. This is ironic. Of all the plans presented here, the Fourth Plan is by far the least practical for general worship. It separates people by great distances. It makes seeing and hearing difficult. It inhibits most forms of liturgy by eliminating the possibility of participation, so why is it so popular?—why is something so unfunctional considered the norm? Perhaps because it was so ideally suited to monasteries, and in the Dark Ages it was the monastic communities that kept the faith alive, so this was the only model to survive. The vast majority of churches today have inherited a central aisle, but very few of these evoke Sacred Journey. That is because the Way requires an expression of extension rather than termination, and such open-ness is rarely found. Also, of all the ministries, Dedication makes the most stringent demands of a congregation, requiring of them commitment, discipline, and self-sacrifice—this is not a ministry for the faint-hearted, nor is it or for the casual church-goer.

This gives rise to an interesting paradox. Churches based on the plan of Sacred Journey are often created by those who are most burdened by tradition, by those most constrained by the full weight of the dead hand of the past, by those who are fearful of trying something new, and by those who believe they know what is "right". And yet Sacred Journey itself is a venture into the unknown. We depart from what is familiar into uncharted territory. We set aside all unnecessary burdens, just carrying with us what is essential to our journey: faith and works.

Some contemporary architects have created magnificent "contemporary relics"—churches with long narrow naves and high echoing vaults—as an invocation of Sacred Journey; churches that by virtue of their poor acoustics and long sight-lines are almost unusable. Some of these churches represent Sacred Journey in a way their architects had never intended: the people have left!

Has technology shaped liturgy? The long narrow spaces of many medieval churches required processions as a means of bringing the performers closer to the audience, at least for the brief moment when they passed down the aisle. This form of space therefore encourages processional crosses, monstrances, banners, vergers, and all manner of portable sanctity. The great distances require chanting, intoning, and plainsong so the Word can be projected beyond the range of speech, and sanctus bells to communicate even further. Could Liturgy be expressed and understood as a response to geometry?

*The Fourth Plan has energy, but there is also sadness.*

*We are on the move.*
*We have left our safe harbor and there is no place for us to stay.*

*foxes have their lairs,*
*birds have their nests,*
*but there is no place for the Son of Man to lay his head.*

*The Fourth Plan is the Plan of Dedication.*
*Go with God.*

The Fourth Plan
## Canadian National War Memorial, Vimy, France
Walter Allward, Architect, 193

FIGURE 72. The Canadian National War Memorial at Vimy.

Twin towers frame a rising space, a route-march to the sky for those Canadian troops who made the supreme sacrifice in the First World War. Most war memorials and cenotaphs are stone columns, sometimes topped-off with a cross. They anchor us firmly to the grave. I know of no other memorial with a central space that inspires us by celebrating in this way the dedication of those who undertook this sacred journey

## Trinity College Chapel, University of Toronto.
### Sir Giles Gilbert Scott, Architect, 1953.

Scott's greatest work, and one of the twelve most beautiful buildings in North America. Most of Scott's works were in a heavy-handed and ponderous Gothic: here Gothic is interpreted with grace and lightness.

This chapel fulfils, precisely, all the requirements for Sacred Journey. The entrance and narthex are at an upper level. A wide flight of steps descends into the chapel. It is like coming down from a mountain and entering a valley. Valleys are linear, a place to journey, as opposed to mountain tops which are discrete places to arrive. At the moment of entering the chapel, as we stand at the top of the steps, we see our whole journey laid out before us.

The chapel is very long, very high, and very narrow. The form of the space bespeaks journey. The walls are in pale tones of grey with repetitive pilasters to mark our progress on our way, but nothing is so arresting as to cause us to stop.

The chancel is marked by a single step.

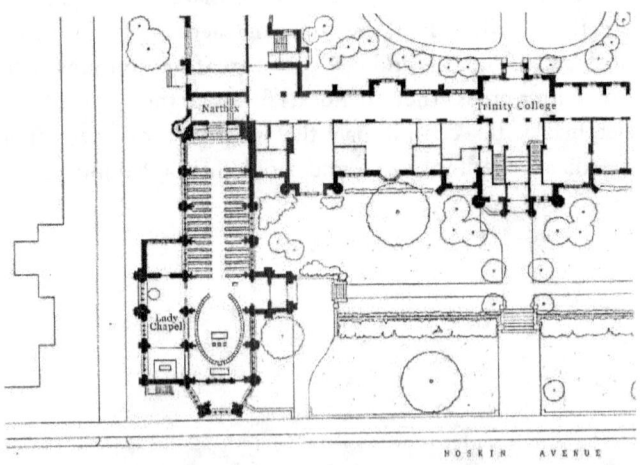

FIGURE 73, Plan of Trinity College at the University of Toronto (the exterior is illustrated in Figure 19, page 37).

FIGURE 74. The Chapel of Trinity College' Toronto, showing how the Way extends to the chancel, to the pierced altar screen, through the apse, and beyond.

The point at which the chapel ends is left ambiguous, as Sacred Journey is not to be confused with arrivals. The chancel is marked by a single step.

An open-work table altar is placed in the center of the chancel, and beyond that the original stone altar can be seen. The stone altar is relatively heavy, but of the same stone as the screen in front of which it stands, and into which it merges.

The screen is pierced with openings through which we can see the apse. The apse has much glass, but it is a clear figured glass which permits light to pass but clouds a vision of the trees beyond. So we are left with no clear statement as to where the space ends. Is it at the chancel step, the table alter, the stone altar, the screen, the apse, the window, or outside? Wherever we look, the end is elsewhere. This carefully-wrought ambiguity, by refusing to end the space at a definite point, allows the linear quality of Sacred Journey to extend beyond our vision. This is evidence of a master at work.

In the pews the people, while still on the journey, listen to the word, recite the prayers, and sing the hymns, in an ordered formation. Then for the Eucharist they move up into the chancel and gather in a circle around the altar where the elements of bread and wine are set out. The candles bid them welcome as they pause to share in the heavenly feast. Then, rested and refreshed, they file out of the church to resume their chosen pilgrimage through time and space.

The final felicity is that the chapel serves a university community. We know we will be together for just a short while as we journey together for a common purpose. Soon we will graduate, separate, and form new relationships in new places. But while we are together we have the Eucharist as our strength and Sacred Journey as our purpose.

## The Fourth Plan
# Abbey Church of Gethsemani, Trappist, Kentucky.
William Shickel, Architect, 1962.

In 1848 a group of monks from the monastery of Melleray in Brittany set sail for the New World. Their pilgrimage took them to rural Kentucky where they established a Trappist community. There they built simple and logical buildings for their community, almost in the Shaker tradition. And in the center of their community they built a church whose steeple punctured the skyline in exactly the same way as they remembered at Melleray. From early photographs it is difficult to tell whether the scene depicted is in Brittany or Kentucky.

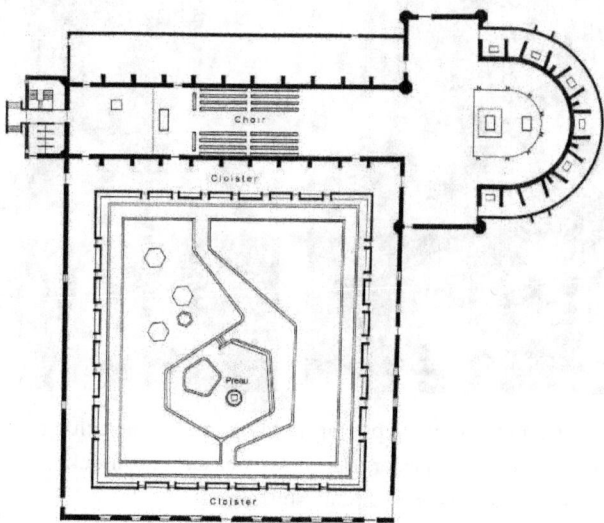

FIGURE 75. The plan of the Abbey Church of Gethsemani in Kentucky retains its original and traditional form.

For these monks Sacred Journey was an extraordinary experience that was now over, and Kentucky was where they had arrived. In their church they were looking for an expression of permanence, and for them permanence meant something that was reminiscent of the historic church they had left behind them and would never see again. However they could not create an authentic Gothic church, all that ornate stonework and carving would be beyond their capabilities. So they built, inside a structural shell, a lath-and-plaster reproduction of the interior of a Gothic church, an extraordinary and unexpected illusion. This was valuable for the original monks, but it served subsequent generations less well. The dark and mysterious interior did not express any of the vitality of the present community which operates a prize-winning farm, sings the daily office, manufactures cheese, fruit cake and chocolate fudge, celebrates the mass, publishes books, pursues theological studies, produces alfalfa pellets, and hosts retreats.

FIGURE 76. Stripping away the plaster moldings and false vaulting (left) reveals an austere and authentic interior (right) to better serve the monks at Gethsemani Abbey. Clear glass windows let the sun shine in.

In 1968 the community engaged architect William Schickel to study their needs. I do not know what was more extraordinary: the fact that Schickel recommended to them tearing out all the ornate plasterwork to get back to a plain interior, or the fact that the community accepted that recommendation! This was matched by the outer drama of the steeple being carried away in a storm.

At any rate, the plaster moldings and imitation vaulting were stripped away. This revealed a beautiful and spare interior with both strength and serenity. The plain brick walls are painted white, the trusses in the roof are of dark wood, and the lancet windows are again rectangular and are glazed with a slightly tinted glass. The space divides naturally into two areas, representing Journey and arrival. Matthew Kelty[53], a member of the community, in fact he is the cobbler, wrote:

> "The long narrow nave is virile. Indeed the notion of an army on the march comes to mind at once; for the stalls themselves have a military stance and the long narrow windows above surely are as good banners as any cause marched beneath ... The whole sweeps forward in a kind of enthusiastic surge, carrying one along in this journey to Jerusalem.
>
> "If the choir and nave is the Way, the sanctuary by contrast is the Arrival, the goal reached. It is in the round, the seating arranged at random about the table where the Lord's Supper is celebrated. This is the place for the memorial meal where the linen is spread, where the family gathers for the breaking of the bread and the drinking of the cup. One can sense the mother, the heart. This is the heavenly church, the city attained, and there is a wholeness, a completion, a gathering of all mankind around the eternal altar for the messianic feast."

A description of Sacred Journey has never been better put.

---

52. Kelty, Gethsemani Renovation.

Rebuilding the Church

## Temporary Chapel for Les Diaconesses de Saint-Loup, Pompales, Switzerland.
Localarchitecture Architects, 2008.

The Community of Deaconesses of St. Loup, a Protestant nursing order, was founded in 1852 in Pompaples, Switzerland, a village some twenty kilometers north of Lausanne. Up to that time virtually all nursing care had been provided to the community by Catholic nuns, so there was much heated discussion among Lutherans and Calvinists about how to create a Protestant equivalent. Should the nurses be Protestant nuns? Should they wear habits? If so, what would be the politically correct color? And the biggest issue of all: should they take vows of obedience? Perhaps that would be too Romish, but perhaps an Order could not survive without such an ordinance.

It all seems to have worked out—the order is flourishing. The deaconesses in their cheerful blue habits provide nursing care in an adjacent hospital. They host seminars and retreats through a "Mountain of Prayer" ministry, offering counseling, intercessions and companion prayer. They have a presence on the internet, and one can enroll on-line.

The community is based in Saint-Loup, overlooking the village of Pompaples, and is named for the nearby Cave of Saint-Loup, possibly the former residence of St. Lupus, who was Bishop of Troyes in 426. He was obliged to become a hermit for a couple of years while he outlived the disgrace of backing the wrong side politically; in his case he consorted with Atilla the Hun, who after some initial successes fell into disfavor, and the Bishop with him.

The mother house is a listed historic building on a mountainous site that has views of the Matterhorn, but over the years time has taken its toll and the building needs substantial renovation. To effect this the deaconesses have found alternate accommodation, but there was no alternate worship space available. The prospect of using a tent or a trailer for a couple of years did not appeal to them in view of the climate, so they instituted a competition for the design of a temporary structure. A firm from nearby Lausanne, Localarchitecture, produced the winning design, a tent-like structure of folded plywood that sits lightly on the ground.

Plywood is manufactured in sheets, and as flexible sheets may be stiffened by being folded or corrugated, by hindsight it seemed natural

PHOTO © MILO KELLER /WWW.MILOKELLER.COM

FIGURE 77. A plywood shell structure creates an elegant temporary enclosure for the Deaconesses. The open-ness at each end enables Sacred Journey to continue out into the world beyond.

to develop the form for such a building by origami, transforming a two-dimensional material into a three-dimensional form. By much tugging and tweaking of many sheets of paper a form was created which is a wonderful evocation of Sacred Journey. As a reward for faith and courage the deaconesses have achieved the finest realization of the Fourth Plan anywhere, and this in an inexpensive plywood structure. The vaults of sloping plywood arch over the Way. Alternately they catch the light so they represent a succession of lights and darks. The space narrows and rises as we approach the altar, a huge directional arrow for the way forward—and as we approach the altar we see the Way extending out into the world through glazed screens tempered with copper mesh. The final felicity is that this chapel is for an intentional community with a vocation of Dedication, which is the ministry associated with the Fourth Plan. The spare, plain interior is not just unfurnished, it depicts emptiness, it is taut with energy referencing back to a geometry that measures the earth, as in the Mary Chapel illustrated in FIGURE 36.

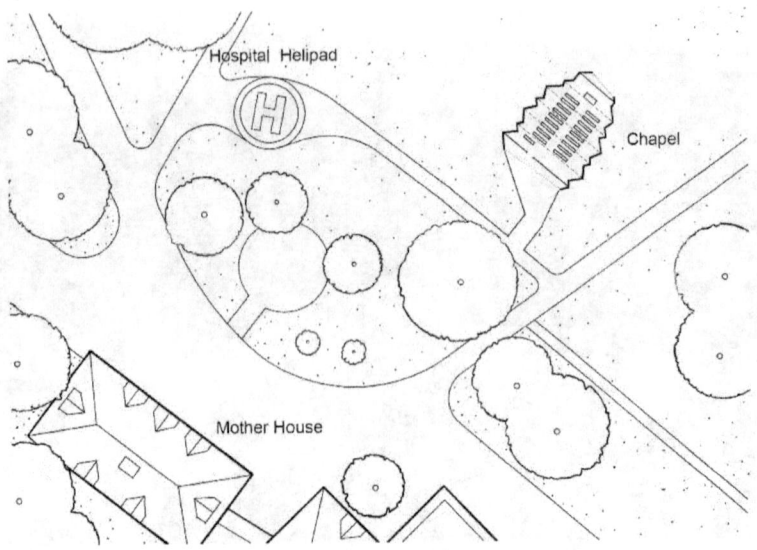

FIGURE 78. Plan of the tiny chapel for the Communauté des Diaconesses de Saint-Loup in Switzerland, a temporary structure of folded plywood.

FIGURE 79. Folded plywood vaults arch over the Way.

## The Fourth Plan

The space is not cluttered with holy hardware, even the altar is transparent. There is no excess baggage to weigh us down on our pilgrimage, and soon the Chapel itself will disappear, to be taken apart and put to a new use in a new place, leaving no trace.

I am including on the next page (figure 80) a diagram of the folds that will create a tiny model of this temporary chapel. The interior space bulges a bit towards the middle, creating a subtle sense of place for us on our journey, holding us as in a pair of cupped hands. The concave walls (as viewed from the interior) by the discipline of origami, create an equally convex roof which is lower at the center but whose height accelerates as it rushes past our little community and out into the world. By directing our attention both upwards and outwards the space affirms a commitment to both faith and works. The pure geometry that created this form is just as strict as the interlocking circles and triangles[54] that generated the plan of the cathedral at Chartres. Just as much meticulous attention to detail was required to create these pristine plain surfaces as in other locations would be needed to create surfaces covered with decoration. The spirit has seeped into the stones, or in this case, into the plywood. This structure is truly a masterpiece. Schwarz would have loved it.

53. Vilette, Chartres, Hasard ou Stricte Géométrie?

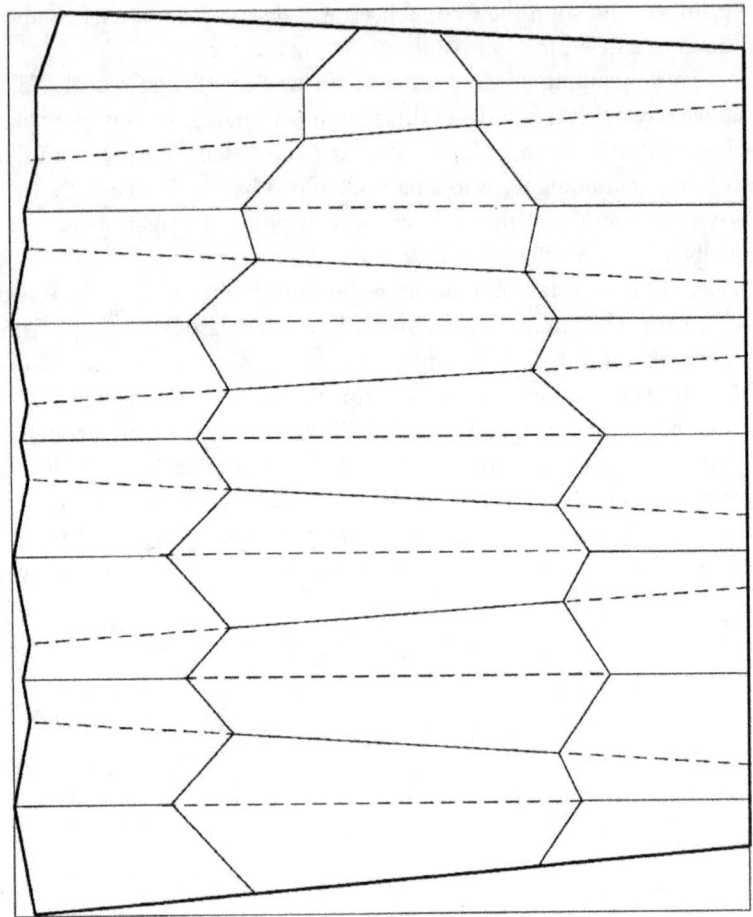

FIGURE 80. Origami unfolded. The form of the space in the tiny chapel may be generated by folding a sheet of paper—the solid lines are mountain folds and the dashed lines are valley folds. A 200% enlargement of the diagram will just fit on to a 8½" x 11" or A4 sheet of paper, which may then be cut and folded to yield the form.

# Chapter 9: The Fifth Plan *for* the Ministry of Evangelism

### The Open Chalice

*A space opens to those on the journey.*
*and the travelers are welcomed*

*The Fifth Plan opens itself,*
*offering shelter to those on the Journey,*
*a Journey that continues.*

The walls of the space curve round behind the altar, enclosing and protecting it. The shape of the walls is a parabola, the same curve as is used in the reflector of a searchlight. The lights on the altar reflect from these walls and form a beam of light shining down the path the pilgrims are taking. The end wall of the space is transparent, so the people can see the lights when they are yet far off. Parabolic reflectors are also used in telescopes which gather-in the light from distant stars.

Guided by the light, the people enter the space and gather round the altar. As they share in the sacraments they forge themselves into a community. When they have received the sacraments and they turn around to return to their places, they see how the lights on the altar continue to shine down, and become, the Way. As they take this shining path out into the world they again become individuals, where they meet and greet other wanderers and invite them too to return with them and share in the feast.

The Open Chalice is one of the most difficult plans for the architect to handle. The problem is that we need a large transparent wall at the west end of the space to open the space to those approaching, and this means that the west end of the space will be brighter than the east end where the altar is. We cannot put a lot of glass in the curved wall because this wall is required to reflect back the light of the altar, not to transmit light. So the danger of this plan is that as one gets closer and closer to the altar the space gets darker and darker. This is what happens in Coventry Cathedral; a space we will be studying later.

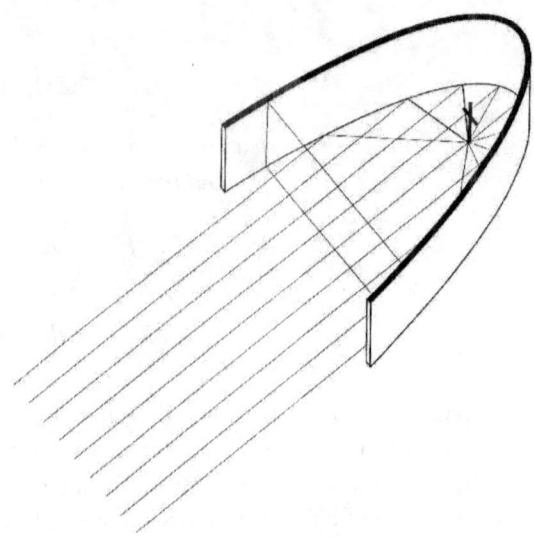

FIGURE 81. The Fifth Plan: the Open Chalice, for the ministry of Evangelism.

The architect has to resort to many measures to correct this situation. The best is to give the altar multi-mega candle power, so it shines out like a beacon down the Way. Perhaps it is possible to shade the glass at the entrance with a canopy, or to use a tinted glass, or to set a transparent screen inside the glass to temper the incoming light while preserving visual transparency. Perhaps there are other ways of introducing light into the interior. These measures all call for careful judgment.

What should happen is that as one moves through the space, from the entrance to the altar, exterior light should become attenuated, and light from the altar should become more intense, and the general brightness should gradually increase, so one feels one is approaching the light rather than leaving it. Entering Coventry Cathedral is like entering a cave: we leave the light at the door.

In the Fifth Plan the voyagers find a safe harbor, not a permanent berth. The parabolic form of the space, the combination of searchlight and telescope, implies movements both inward and outward. It accepts the travelers, nurtures them sets them on their way. This form of space is appropriate for those whose focus is evangelism. The people move out into the world to share the Good News and bring the World to the Sacrament. In doing this they put themselves at risk, because the world does not always want to hear them. But some do, and those who do are invited to come back to meet, join and work with the community. The Fifth Plan is at the center of a lot of activity in the world—much coming and going.

Evangelism is intimate, a personal invitation to share in the gifts of the spirit. It requires a one-on-one contact and involves risk. Most self-proclaimed evangelists using lecture halls or the air-waves are in fact practicing Witness; a much more aloof, authoritarian, and safe ministry. They do not venture out on to the Way to meet those seeking a path. Rather, supported by a large and expensive staff, they ascend into high places and shout in the hope that someone will hear them. If we experience Evangelism as a struggle for dominance over others we are doing it wrong in both senses of the word. The Open Chalice receives, blesses and releases. The Fifth Plan is the home church for missionaries, teachers and greeters, those who take seriously Christ's instruction to grow the church. Without wallet and staff they are out on the Way, guiding and welcoming. We are delighted when they spend some time with us, and yet we know their work is elsewhere.

Rebuilding the Church

## The Church of St. George the Martyr, Toronto
Gerald Robinson Architect, 1986

Originally there was a large 1845 Victorian Gothic church on this site in downtown Toronto, overlooking a park. A fire destroyed it in 1955, leaving just the tower standing. As a practical measure the old parish hall was converted for use as worship space, but this left the community without space for its other ministries.

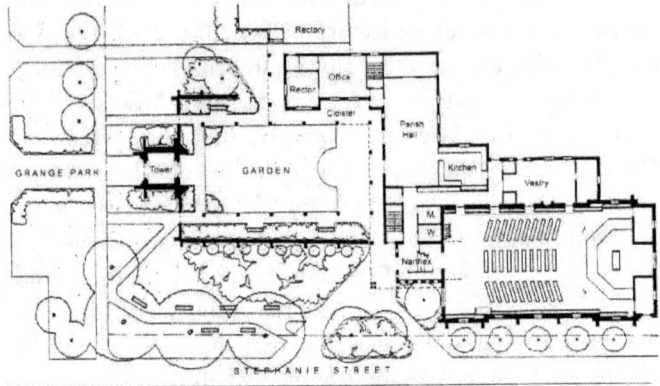

FIGURE 82. Plan of the Church of St. George the Martyr, Toronto. The ghost image of the old church can be seen in the brickwork of the surviving tower, and in the walls that surround the garden. The free-standing columns in the garden are set on the foundations of those that once supported the roof.

Thirty years later, in a program to restore this functionality, the foundations of the old church were uncovered and walls were built on these foundations to create an enclosed garden (see figs. 83 and 84) where the nave used to be. A ministry building containing parish office, Sunday school, residences and a fellowship room was built partially on the foundations of the old church, with a cloister (figure 84) tying together all the buildings on the site.

This church is an expression of the Fifth Plan. French doors with clear glass reveal the altar from the narthex. The walls of beige brick are not parabolic but they do however wrap round behind the altar and open up towards the west.

FIGURE 83. In the evening the garden hosts a wedding reception in an area that was once the nave of the former church, of which only the tower survives. Monoliths mark the placement of the former columns. One may now find oneself in the church without entering the church.

Most of the daylight comes from the west end of the church where there is a large gothic window (rescued from another church) glazed with clear glass. Windows in the south wall are smaller and the window behind the altar is of stained glass so we have the feature that the level of lighting from outside decreases as we move to the east. To balance this, the altar is illuminated quite brightly so the overall level of illumination is fairly uniform as one source takes over from the other.

Here we embody the four criteria for the Fifth Plan:

> 1. The altar is visible from the outside,

> 2. The walls surrounding the altar open up to the people.

> 3. The daylight of the world is gradually replaced by the light of the spirit, and most importantly

> 4. Entering the space is easy, and acknowledges the Way.

# Rebuilding the Church

### Expressing the Way

In the case of this church the Way is not a journey through the world, it is a journey through human development; the path we have trod to become the people we are. The five stages of the journey are through the Street, the Park, the Garden, the Narthex, and the Sanctuary.

FIGURE 84. Columns built over the foundations of the old church (the grass area is the former nave) support a new ministry building and form a cloister that ties the whole development together.

The Way begins in our world, the Way of the street. The street is created for the movement of cars, trucks, people, bicycles, buses. Overhead are channels for electric power and electronic communication. Below it are channels for the flow of water, sewage and gas. The street is a completely mechanistic system. We are not yet in the church. Some people live their entire lives at the level of Street, driven by pressures and constrained by channels.

From the street we enter Grange Park. Parks are created entirely for pleasure. Flowers are tended for their beauty, trees for their shade, grass for recreation, benches for rest. All is laid out for enjoyment. Some people live their entire lives at the level of Park, focusing all their attention on pleasure and comfort.

## The Fifth Plan

From the park we enter the garden. The garden was created out of the shell of the former church. This is the space where people have worshiped for over a hundred years. Here we can make contact with our Judeo-Christian heritage and the Old Religion which preceded it. In part of the garden wall there is a columbarium to receive the ashes of those who have gone before, so there is expressed a continuity with former members of the community. The cloister is reminiscent of those monastic communities that kept the faith alive through dark times. Some of the columns of the old church are left standing in the garden, silent monoliths that recall the works of the Old Religion. In the garden it is possible for us to relate to our heritage. Some people spend their entire life at the level of Garden, focused on the old, rejecting the new, and regretting the passing of the past.

From the garden we enter the narthex. This forms an entry to the new Mission Building, a facility for education, counseling and community. This is where our work is. Some people spend their entire lives at the level of Narthex, busy with work for the structures and administration of the community, without regard for expression of the self.

FIGURE 85. The Church of St. George the Martyr welcomes all who enter.

From the narthex we can see the candles on the altar in the sanctuary. We enter and approach. The walls stretch out their arms to welcome us, the light beckons. We turn our backs to the world as we approach the altar. We receive the Host with our companions on the Way. As soon as this is accomplished we turn around, and there we see our work in front of us, waiting for us.

The evangelical ministry of the church is reflected in its open-ness to the surrounding community. There is no hard edge between street and sanctuary—the one merges seamlessly into the other. A minister reported that the garden sees more activity now than the space did a century ago when it was the nave of the old church. Every day workers from the surrounding office towers arrive with their lunch in paper bags, mothers with small children spread their blankets on the grass, and in the evenings there are concerts, recitals, picnics, wedding receptions, and sometimes outdoor worship. The church stands at the center of a network of ministries. Bible classes are held in surrounding homes and the church offers spiritual counseling courses. It trains and supports evangelical teams in the parish and missionaries overseas. A world map in the narthex, stuck with stick-pins, indicates the extent of the outreach of the church to such places as Nigeria and El Salvador; an outreach which is symbolized by the opening walls of the Fifth Plan.

The Fifth Plan

## Coventry Cathedral

Sir Basil Spence, Architect, 1951.

Over the years three cathedrals have stood on this site, and there have been an equal number of destructions. The first cathedral was part of the Benedictine Priory of St. Mary, established in 1043 by Leofric, Earl of Mercia, and his more famous wife, the Lady Godiva. The cathedral was built on the site of a nunnery founded by St. Osburga circa 700 AD which was sacked by Edric the Traitor in 1016. The Dissolution of the Monasteries promulgated by King Henry VIII caused the cathedral to be abandoned and fall into ruin in 1539. Some of its masonry was plundered for other buildings in the town. In 1918 a new cathedral (known today as "the old cathedral") was proclaimed as a new role for the sixteenth-century St. Michael's Church. This survived until 1940, when a rain of firebombs in the war cause a conflagration which left just a few stone walls standing. Some saw the later Allied fire-bombing of Dresden as a reprisal for this.

The day after the bombing it was decided to rebuild the cathedral as a center for reconciliation and unity. Sir Giles Gilbert Scott, who was later to be the Architect for the new Trinity College Chapel in Toronto (figure 74, page 141), created a plan in which a new cathedral with a long high nave extended north from the existing ruins. However his plan was rejected by the Royal Fine Arts Commission for its antiquarian character, so it was decided to hold an architectural competition for the new cathedral. Out of two hundred entries the competition was won by Basil Spence with a modernist interpretation of the Gothic Style. He retained the relationship with the ruins proposed by Scott, and linked the two structures with a huge covered porch. His design was controversial, causing a lot of adverse comment in the architectural press who felt the design was compromised by its stylistic references, and a more frankly contemporary design should have been chosen.

The plan of Coventry Cathedral has obvious affinities with the Fifth Plan illustrated in Figure 81. Masonry walls wrap around behind the altar and become wider as they extend towards the entrance. The entrance wall is a huge sheet of glass. Narrow windows in the side walls are angled in the manner of louvers to direct light on the altar.

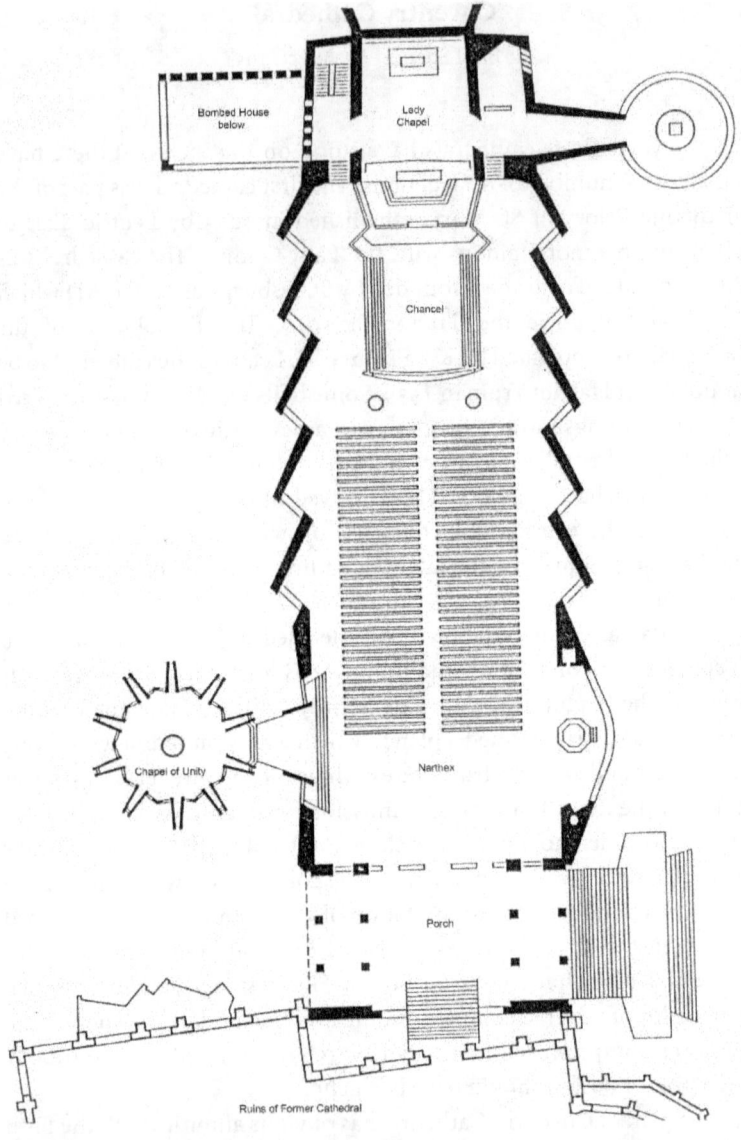

FIGURE 86. Plan of Coventry Cathedral. A covered porch connects the new cathedral with the bombed-out shell of the old one.

There are also similarities with the Church of St. George the Martyr (figure 82) in Toronto, in that access to the cathedral is made through.

the ruins of a previous church that had been destroyed by fire The description of the various stages of the Way which was given for the Church of St. George the Martyr could apply equally to Coventry Cathedral.

From this we could assume that the plan of the cathedral could support the liturgies and forms of worship associated with the Open Chalice. In fact there are some practical difficulties, mainly centering around the light.

FIGURE 87. The glare and gloom of Coventry Cathedral's vast cave-like nave, which functions as a narthex for tourists, pilgrims, and visitors.

The entrance screen consists of huge panels clear glass on which are engraved images of fashionably emaciated saints and anorexic angels, the work of John Hutton, This screen admits so much light there is no way of balancing it with interior illumination. The side windows are of no help at all. They are of traditional stained glass, designed by Laurie Lee, and are so heavily overpainted they are darker than the walls. The architect lost control of his artists. They were off on a frolic of their own, each doing his own thing instead of submitting to the discipline of a common purpose, and this scatter shows up in the final work. Many have commented on this, and have said harsh things about the cathedral because the glare at the entrance and the gloom at the altar make the space unsuitable for the Eucharist; a cave rather than a chalice.

Now we have to remember that the Open Chalice is designed to support the ministry of Evangelism. Is this the ministry of Coventry Cathedral? From everything that has been said and written by those responsible for its operation, and by everything we can observe ourselves, clearly it is not.

## The Ministry of Coventry

On the day after the bombing it was decided to rebuild the cathedral as a center for reconciliation and unity. That message comes through very powerfully to every visitor. It is very clear that this is the purpose of the cathedral. Forgiveness has to start with the one offended. A cross made from the charred beams of the old cathedral, with the inscription "Father Forgive", has been visited by hundreds of thousands. The Cross of Nails, made from ancient nails recovered from the burnt timbers, has been distributed all over the world. Many nations have assisted with the reconstruction, including the nation that sourced the destruction. The purpose, thrust, and ministry of Coventry Cathedral is Reconciliation.

Reconciliation is a form of Pastoral Care. This is the ministry supported by the Second Plan: Sacred Meeting. How well does the Second Plan fit the structure at Coventry? The Second Plan expresses a duality of space; a large open space for the people and a smaller, more-enclosing space for the altar, and free-and-open access between the two. The nave at Coventry forms a large open space, large enough for visitors by the bus-load. For the smaller space there are two possibilities: the Chapel of Unity and a diorama in the crypt. The nave then functions more like a narthex, a gathering place. A narthex often contains a bulletin board, postcards from parishioners, odd items rescued from the archives and put on display for the enlightenment of visitors, sales of cookbooks compiled by the ladies of the parish, a short history of the church, and assorted tracts. In "A place to Loiter" Ginny Maurepas[55] writes: "In the early church the narthex had the role of the donut shoppe in present society, but without the twenty minute time limit."

---

54. Maurepas, A Place to Loiter.

## The Fifth Plan

The nave of Coventry Cathedral works very well as a narthex. The people are entertained while they wait. They can see the world's biggest tapestry. They can see a font made out of a boulder from the Holy Land, an eighty-foot stained glass window by John Piper and Patrick Reyntiens, and a bust of Christ made out of the metal from a crashed car. Marchita Mauck[56] has commented:

> "Visitors tour the church as they would a museum of post-war English art. One leaves having no strong impression that this is a place in which an assembly gathers for prayer. One imagines rather an endless procession of tourists moving from object to object, explanatory brochures in hand, like a perpetual stations of the cross."

This would be a scathing review, and it is only one of many others, if it were describing the sanctuary of a cathedral. As a description of a narthex however, it seems perfectly appropriate. The narthex is very large, very open, and sometimes it accommodates religious and theatrical performances.

Of the smaller spaces, the Chapel of Unity, Figure 88, is devoted to healing the schisms and divisions in the church and in the world. The chapel stands on land held in trust for this purpose; it is the common property of all who wish to share in this mission[57]. At the threshold is a stone bearing the inscription "That All Shall Be One". The smallness of this space is confronting: it implies that not too many people are interested in unity.

The other small space, Figure 89, is a diorama of a typical bombed house. It is set at a lower level. One descends stairs, as many seeking protection have done. We hear a recording of planes overhead, and distant gunfire. The house bespeaks a human presence, as if the occupants have just left, or have just been taken away. It brought back to life some of my own wartime experiences in London, and I am sure for others it was reminiscent of Beirut, or Cologne. It communicates a determination that this cannot be allowed to happen again.

---

55. Mauck, Ambiguity and Paradox.

56. Williams, Coventry Cathedral.

FIGURE 88. Two shrines at Coventry: the tiny Chapel of Unity...

FIGURE 89. ...and in the crypt, a representation of a bombed house.

## The Fifth Plan

As an expression of reconciliation the sequence of spaces at Coventry Cathedral works well. An axis depicting the Way transects the ruins of the Old Cathedral and enters the New. In this case the Way leads out of a thousand years of conflict and destruction represented by the old ruins, and into a place for the gathering of men and women of goodwill, where they can find inspiration and promise to heal divisions and make a difference in the world. This is the noble purpose for the cathedral. The cathedral does not intend to be the worship center for a Eucharistic community performing the liturgies of a particular denomination; that is the function of the adjacent Holy Trinity Church. To quote the Provost[58] (and he should know):

> "Holy Trinity is the great parish church in the center of the city, and its work and the cathedral's are entirely and happily complementary."

Coventry Cathedral has been assailed by architectural aesthetes since the day it was built, criticizing it for not being what it is not. All this time it has been immensely popular with the public, who enjoy it for what it is. Its major space, conforming to the Fifth Plan, welcome visitors, tourists and strangers. Few of these are expected to join a regular congregation here, but all will be influenced by the message of peace and reconciliation.

---

57. Williams, Coventry Cathedral.

REBUILDING THE CHURCH

## Kirche zum Heilig-Kreuz, Bottrop, Ruhr, Germany.
Rudolf Schwarz, Architect, 1952 –57.

The Heilig-Kreuz church in the coal-mining town of Bottrop appears to be a physical manifestation of Rudolf Schwarz's Fifth Plan. How could that be? Schwarz was quite clear that the Six Plans were theoretical representations of ideas about space and worship, they were not documents to be used for the construction of buildings, and Schwarz himself never used any of these Plans for any of his own church buildings. However Father Wilhelm Eilers, the parish priest for this coal-mining community and the force behind the building of this church in Bottrop, had already read Schwarz's 1938 book *Vom Bau der Kirche* and was much taken with the form of the Fifth Plan, so when he selected Schwarz as his architect he also selected the Fifth Plan as the plan for his new church. Schwarz objected strongly to this misuse of his concept, and the church authorities too objected to this proposal, but the priest was adamant.

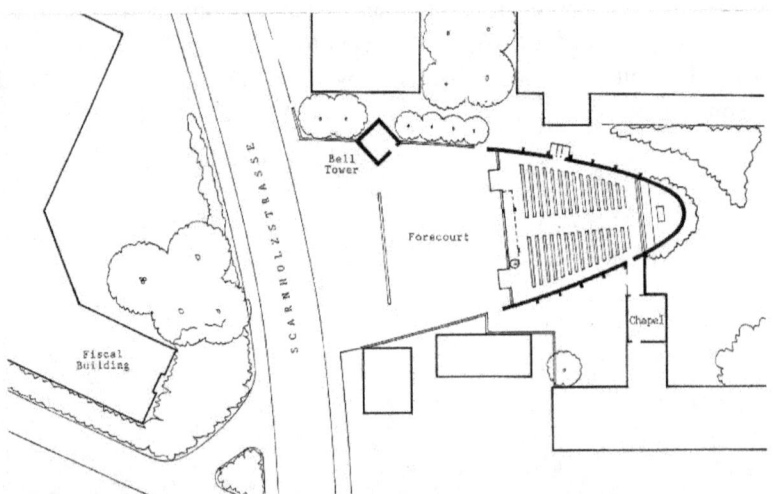

FIGURE 90. One of the Six Plans that got built, Compare this plan for the Heilig Kreuz church in Germany with the archetypal Open Chalice plan in figure 81.

The closeness of the correspondence of the church to the Fifth Plan can be seen by comparing the plan of the church with the archetypal plan as

## The Fifth Plan

illustrated in Figure 81. They have in common a parabolic plan for the space, a transparent glazed screen at the west end, and wing-walls that project beyond the screen to open up the church in a gesture of welcome. The altar is in a free-standing location at the focal point of the parabolic arc as demanded by the geometry of the plan instead of being set up against the end wall as was the tradition at that time. This separation enabled Fr. Eilers to celebrate the mass while facing the people, which he did despite the objections of his bishop. However, six years later, the Second Vatican Council decreed that all Catholic churches should move their altars away from the rear wall and all priests should face the people when celebrating the mass, so a *deus ex machina* resolved this dispute.

The essential feature if the Fifth Plan is the easy coming-and-going of the people. This is the plan that welcomes pilgrims and sends them on their way. In Bottrop the welcome is expressed by the glazed entrance screen which expresses the open-ness of the interior to those still outside. It bears a huge spiral pattern of stained glass by Georg Meistermann.

FIGURE 91. The impressive glazed screen for the Heilig Kreuz church, through which can be seen . . .

FIGURE 92 ... an interior of great strength, calm, and integrity.

The spiral is even more impressive from within, where its red-and-orange-decked swirls can be appreciated. It imposes a vast cosmic form on the view of the outside world. This, together with the extending wing-walls, illustrates a church reaching out into the secular world, reaching out as Christ reaches out to humanity. This welcoming of the World to the Sacrament is the fundamental relationship of the Fifth Plan.

## The Fifth Plan

The interior of the church is impressive in its simplicity. The exposed brickwork of the interior gives the impression of being unfinished, of being stripped down to reveal fundamental truths. This clear simplicity, which extends to the church furnishings and appointments, creates an interior of clarity, austerity, and peace. The photograph of the interior, Figure 92, serves to illustrate the proposition, given in the first chapter, that space is not visual—we feel space in our bodies, we do not see it with our eyes. The photograph depicts an interior that we might consider visually gloomy, perhaps even a bit claustrophobic, but that is not what is felt by the occupants. What the people experience, and what the camera cannot reveal, is that behind the worshipers there is a vast empty space illuminated by a huge expanse of glazing whose cosmic swirls bathe the whole interior with light, and that spaciousness is part of the experience of being there. The congregation find themselves in a condition of dynamic tension between the Sacrament and the World. The Lord extends his arms in welcome. He offers them the holy gifts, and when they have received them and they turn to leave they see before them the world, in all its chaos and confusion: the world to which they must return.

To accommodate other uses in the space the pews may be moved or removed, and there are marks on the floor to ensure they will be returned to their correct positions. When the space is booked for recitals and rock concerts a light-show splashes colors all over the curving walls, while from way up high the Eye of God looks down on God's children and on what they are doing in God's house.

The Heilig-Kreuz church is one of the churches mentioned in a splendid pocket guide "Modern Architecture in Europe"[59]. When the authors, Dennis and Elizabeth DeWitt, visited this church they remarked that: " . . . like many successful churches, it represents a mingling of the practical with the inexplicable."

They noted all the rational, practical aspects of the construction: the exposed brick, the glazing, the concrete framing, but beyond this, in the realm of the inexplicable, they felt that something special was happening. They felt that this church " . . . is not meant to be just a building, but rather, metaphysically, the knowable fraction of a universal order . . . with some vast extension implied in its projecting walls."

---

58. DeWitt, Modern Architecture in Europe, 86.

Of the over one thousand buildings reviewed by the DeWitts, this small church in a mining town in Northern Germany is the only one where they noted that it extended beyond its actual site, just as Stonehenge and the Pyramids extend beyond their sites in cosmic alignments

It is interesting that the authors contrast the practical and the inexplicable. In these pages we have learned that, for a church, the spiritual is "practical", and there is a rational explanation for "the inexplicable". We have been creating a map for that area of the universal order that extends beyond its knowable fraction.

The DeWitts were so entranced by this church they were moved to offer the poetic metaphor that ".... this church may be not unlike the brilliant perigee of a comet: that brief moment of reflected glory which permits us to surmise the vast extensions of the comet's realm—but without which that realm is none the less real."

Their imagery was perhaps more precise than they had realized. The tail of a comet does not stream out behind it as is often depicted. The tail always points away from the sun, acting as a celestial weather vane to indicate the direction of that stream of low-energy particles pouring out from the sun known as the solar wind[60]. The luminous tail streaming out from the orb for millions of kilometers receives its direction from the sun. In the same manner, the pilgrim way of the Fifth Plan, streaming out from the heart of the Open Chalice, is aligned in its direction by a yet greater Source.

---

59. Moore, *Comets*.

# Chapter 10: The Sixth Plan *for* the Ministry of Justice

**The Dome of Light**

The Sixth Plan is a transparent, open dome.

The people gather round the altar,
but their attention is directed outwards towards the world.

The work of the people is healing the world,
In this they will be scattered through the world,
like seeds.

The dome is transparent. The people can see the world all around them.
The dome focuses their vision.

In the center of the dome is the altar.

Light from the altar shines on the people, illuminates their hearts,
and continues to shine out past them into the world.

The people see a world illuminated by the light from the altar.

The people shine with the Christ-light within them.

When they go into the world they take this light into the world with them.

The world only distantly sees the light from the Dome of Light,
but the world has immediate experience
of the light in the hearts of the people.

It is this Light that can heal the world.
the light which the people take out into the world

The healing of the world by the light of the Eucharist is a recurring theme in the writings of Bishop Arthur Lichtenberger[61], a champion of social causes: "God's light shines in the darkness of the World as it is now, with its disorder and oppression, its violence and injustice. The darkness does not disappear, but in God's light each of us can see enough to be the Church wherever we are. Each time we receive the Body and Blood of our Lord, we are by that act sent out to be witnesses to Him in the world. This does not mean that we are to lead pious lives, but we are to be in the thick of the fight for justice and freedom and peace."

The Dome of Light is an appropriate plan for those seeking change in the world. It is for congregations devoted to support for the environment, care for the suffering, right government for the nation, corporate responsibility, and a just society. It is the plan for those that wrestle with the forces of privilege, prejudice, and oppression.

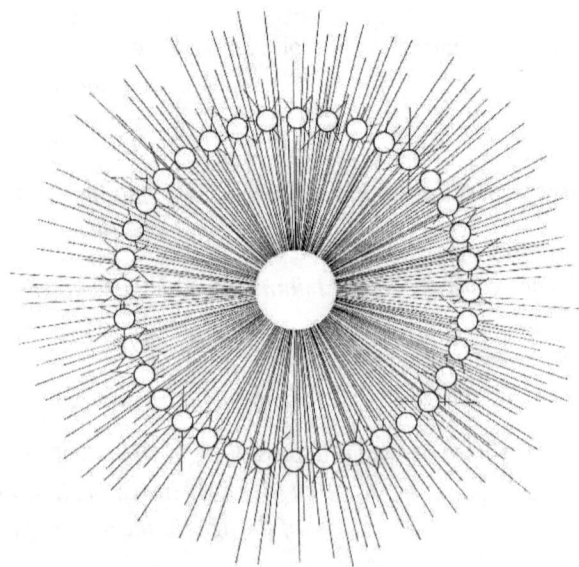

FIGURE 93. The Sixth Plan: the Dome of Light, for the ministry of Justice.

60. Lichtenberger, *The Day is at Hand*.

# The Sixth Plan

The Sixth Plan is the plan for Justice. It is the plan for those who struggle to create a world worthy for the coming of Christ.

The Dome of Light, for which Rudolf Schwarz created such a beautiful drawing seen in Figure 3, page 8, may exist in many forms. Ideally it is a dome of glass, so the light of worship can shine in all directions. It could be a completely open structure, or a structure with openings all around the perimeter, to permit the people carrying the light to venture out into all the world, expressing the relationship of the parameters for the ministry of Justice, where the People stream out into the World. The Dome of Light is the least substantial of all the Six Plans: all that is required is that the light and the people should be able to illuminate the world. In the Dome of Light, Jesus bids us shine.

This is the charge expressed in the closing words of the old Latin mass "Ite, Missa Est", which is poorly translated in the modern rite as "Go forth, the Mass is ended." The Latin phrase carries much more meaning than "It's over, folks. Now you can go home!" The word "Missa", from which the English word "mass" is derived, is the Low Latin form of "missio"[62], meaning a sending forth or a mission. So the final words of the Latin mass had a quality, missing in the English translation, of bidding us to go out into the world and do God's work. In the imagery of Karl Barth the words "Ite, Missa Est" are the hinge[63] where our attention turns from inward to outward, marking the point where our work in the liturgy ends and our work in the world resumes. The hinge is not the door by which we leave the church. The hinge connects while the door separates.

The new prayer book[64] for the Evangelical Lutheran Church bases its rites for Holy Communion on the sequence of Gathering, Word, Meal, and Sending. In "Sending" God blesses us and sends us in mission to the world, with the words:

> "We are sent to continue our participation in God's mission. With the blessing of God, we go out to live as Christ's body in the world."

---

61. Cross, Oxford Dictionary of the Christian Church.

62. Barth, *Epistle to the Romans*. 35

63. Evangelical Lutheran Worship, 93.

The same charge is expressed in the prayer after communion taken from the Book of Alternate Services of the Anglican Church of Canada[65]:

> "May we who share his body
> > live his risen life;
>
> we, who drink his cup,
> > bring life to others;
>
> we, whom the spirit lights,
> > give light to the world."

The Sixth Plan is the plan for engaging with the world to bring forth Justice and Freedom and Peace for all God's creatures.

---

64. Book of Alternate Services, 215.

THE SIXTH PLAN

## Salvation Army Meeting, KwaMashu, Natal, South Africa

This place of worship is both simple and deceptively simple. What factors influenced this spot to be chosen, rather than another? The great cathedrals sprang from such tenuous beginnings. Something special about this particular site caused it to be chosen; and after it had become chosen it became special in another way. Referring to Ancient Greece and Rome, Vitruvius stated "All gathering places under the open sky constitute architectural works." (*De Architectura*, .L5.)

FIGURE 94. The open-ness of the Sixth Plan is demonstrated at a Salvation Army meeting in South Africa.

What we have here is an open-air cathedral.
In South Africa, during the regime of apartheid, KwaMashu, like all the black townships, was a center of unrest. And like all black townships it was located conveniently out of sight of the white centers of population. The townships would be located in the next valley, round the

bend of the river, on the other side of the hill. The citizens of Durban have heard of KwaMashu, in fact they have heard a lot about it, but for the most part they have no direct experience of its existence. This is a Light that they do not see directly. A reflection of this light has to be carried out to them, in the heart.

THE SIXTH PLAN
# The Church of the Holy Trinity, Toronto
Henry Bowyer Lane, Architect, 1847.

The people gather for the Eucharist. They stand round the altar in a circle. The form of worship is not influenced by the cruciform architecture of the church walls, nor by the arrangement of the seating. The format is very much like that for an open-air meeting, if an open-air meeting could be held in a church. The church was built in a traditional cruciform plan, but the shape of the worship is a circle, independent of the shape of the walls. The people are not contained by the walls, they are free: free to take the light of the Eucharist out into the world.

FIGURE 95. The Church of the Holy Trinity, Toronto—not a church without walls, but a church where walls do not set limits on worship.

The church was established to be a church for the poor, "the seats to be free and unappropriated for ever"[66]. This tradition of support for the

---

65. Arthur, Toronto, No Mean City, 84.

underdog has run consistently through the history of the church. This church has had a history of rocking the boat, so its relationships with temporal and ecclesiastical governments have not always been smooth. In fact it has the distinction of having been threatened simultaneously with expropriation by the one authority, and disestablishment by the other.

In the 1930s the Church of the Holy Trinity was a distribution center for used clothing and the Parish Hall was used as a hostel for homeless men. The Rector, who was a member of the City Council, led a vast crowd of the unemployed in a protest march to the Provincial Legislature. He did not get elected to a second term, a result of an anti-communist smear campaign conducted by his opponents.

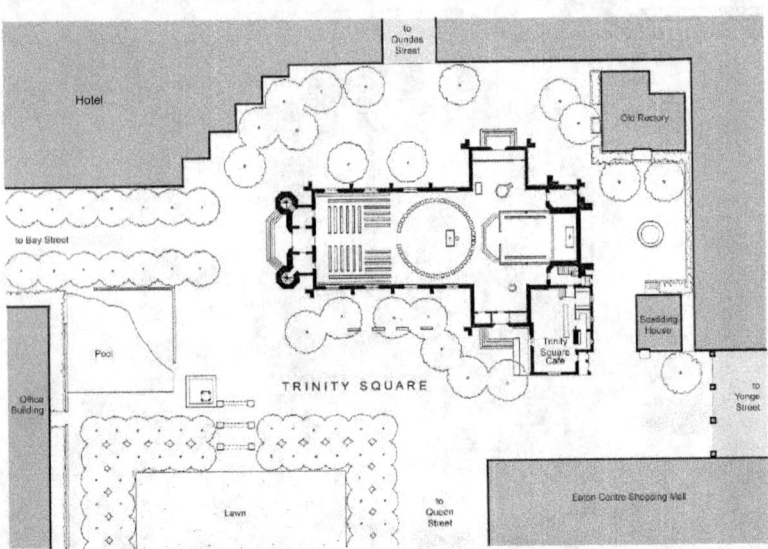

FIGURE 96. Plan of the Church of the Holy Trinity, Toronto, set in a pedestrian precinct in the heart of a downtown commercial redevelopment whose layout was negotiated by the church.

Thirty years later, at the time of the Viet Nam war, hundreds of young people from the United States slept in the church, on their way to making a new life in Canada. The rear half of the church was partitioned off to give the temporary residents a bit of privacy from the worshiping community, but this did not prevent the perfumes of illicit smoking mixtures from one side of the fence mingling with the incense from the other.

FIGURE 97. The Church of the Holy Trinity, set in a pedestrian precinct in the heart of downtown.

The church has had City Councilors and Members of Parliament among its members, usually of a strong reform persuasion. Its members have been prominent in the Peace Movement, the Women's Movement, and the struggle for justice in Central and South America. It provides offices for Amnesty International, for boycotts of various unacceptable products such as the canned milk being marketed by Nestlés to babies of the Third World, and a Distress Center for suicide counseling.

These concerns filter into the worship of the community, which is strongly congregational in character. The liturgy is re-cast in inclusive language, which tempers some of the traditional imagery of masculine domination, so God is referred to at times as "our Father and Mother", continuing a tradition of the fifth-century Celtic Church. Some services are signed for the deaf and the congregation has learned enough sign language to participate in the prayers and responses, which enriches the experience of worship by creating a sort of liturgical dance.

The community gains its strength from a shared Eucharist and this strength is expressed as action in the world.

# Rebuilding the Church

## St. James's Church, Piccadilly, London
Sir Christopher Wren, Architect, 1684.

This is one of the most noted of London's Wren churches; it has had more publicity than any other church in Britain and it was Sir Christopher's favorite.

The church originally fronted on to Jermyn Street, with a large door in the middle of its south wall. In 1848 this door was blocked and a window put in its place. Vestibules were added to the north and south sides of the tower, so the church now faces equally to Jermyn Street and to Piccadilly in London's fashionable West End. It provides a convenient access between Turnbull & Asser and the Ritz Hotel.

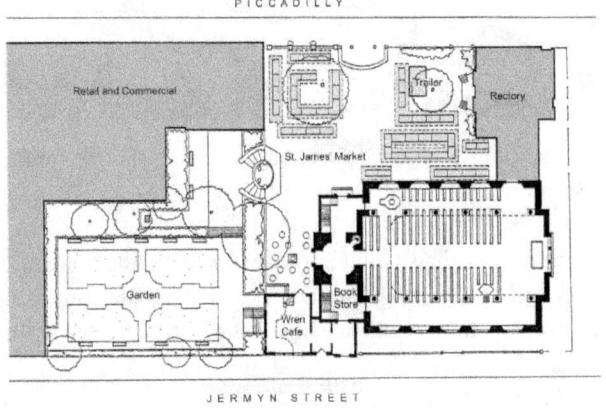

FIGURE 98. Plan of St. James' Church, Piccadilly.

The interior is in the form of one great room with a vaulted ceiling, every part of which is visible at once. Tall windows of clear glass provide light in abundance, in a fine seventeenth-century representation of the Dome of Light. The brightness of the interior and the clarity of its planning, are metaphors for the simplicity and clarity of the faith.

At a deeper level, the entire placement of the church evokes the Dome of Light; a dome that is transparent, invisible and without definite boundary. Between the church and the city there is also no definite

FIGURE 99. The Dome of Light at St. James' Church, Piccadilly. The shell motif of St. James is seen behind the altar.

boundary. True, there is a wrought iron fence and iron gates between the church courtyard and the crowds of Piccadilly, but the gates are open and the courtyard is filled with a street fair, the St. James' Market, where merchants and craftspeople sell their wares and there are even more people in the courtyard than there are on the street. There is a permanently parked trailer, bearing the sign: "St. James' Walk-In Help and Advice Centre", which brings ministry to the market. Such markets[67] were an inseparable part of religious life of the Middle Ages. They were held on those feast days that drew the largest crowds of worshipers. They occupied all the space around the church, and sometimes took up space on the inside as well. The many ordinances passed by Chapters to prevent the loud lusty life of the marketplace from spilling over into the sanctuary show how inseparable the two were in reality.

Approaching the church from the south, from Jermyn Street, we first pass through a café set up in the narthex—a welcoming sight. Thus the trade and commerce which is the main staple of the surrounding

---

66. von Simson, The Gothic Cathedral.

streets extends into the fabric of the church. This makes it very easy to enter the church; at no point is there a sudden change.

FIGURE 100. The approach to St. James' Church is through the patio of a café in the narthex.

The activities of the street continue into the church itself. This gives the message that the church is open to all. To the west of the church there is a garden created out of the old churchyard. This plot, known as God's Garden, is being developed as a sanctuary, with biblical plants, healing herbs and wild flowers. Certain plants are set out as growing prayers and with each prayer a stone is placed on a cairn, at the heart of which is a stone from the Holy Land.

Always there is a large number of visitors. Some, encouraged by such an "open" church, seek baptism and membership in the Anglican Church. The church remains open till midnight on Saturdays and on some occasions, when the weather is bad, it stays open beyond that, as a shelter for the homeless. Visitors are made welcome and invited to stay for a while and those who do so find there are many ministries and programs that offer support. There is a program to explore the meaning of Christian faith and practice. Talks and discussion groups examine our role in the world. A center for health and healing deals with personal well-ness and offers natural therapies, acupuncture, psychotherapy and

# The Sixth Plan

Figure 101. A street market mediates between the church and the city.

spiritual healing. Music and the arts are supported by providing space for performance and exhibition. At Christmas fifty young Christians and Muslims meet in the church for a falafel supper in the nave where they talk and eat and get to know one other. They celebrate Christmas together—the Christian feast celebrating the birth of Jesus who is also honored as a prophet in the Qur'an. The church also hosts a breakfast every week for refugees. They share stories over scrambled eggs, toast, and coffee. All of them want to help themselves, to get a job, to contribute, but it's frustrating that they are not allowed to work.

The Dome of Light permits people to enter with ease from all quarters. The Dome Light also has the function of transmitting the light of the Eucharist out into the world. In fact, the seven major ministries of St. James' are called "lamps".

The church has also provided a platform for The Women of Greenham Common, those perennial protesters of the nuclear presence. Such a stance has caused a lot of criticism to be focused on St. James' Piccadilly, but a former rector, Rev. Donald Reeves, strongly rejected the notion that the Church should be in any way divorced from politics[68], saying:

> "We are making connections between faith and life. People have reduced Christianity to going to church, but Jesus didn't talk about the Church, or even God, but about the Kingdom, about renewing every part of creation. If one was going to believe that the Church is the sole place where god is to be found, then God help the Church, and God help God."

**The Urban Church**

This illustrates how churches in the city center can tackle controversial issues. Since the urban church is not set in a residential community, it does not have to uphold community values; in fact, part of its role is to challenge them.

This is both a strength and a weakness: the weakness is that without a ready-made community surrounding the church, the church itself has

---

67. Billen, The Times, February 26 1987.

to forge the bonds to maintain itself as a community, and this may sap the energy of the congregation. The Rector writes:

> "The traditional structure of a paid professional priest 'leading' about 150 people gathered on a Sunday is entirely inappropriate to the ministry of a city center church. It is not only inappropriate, but it has, in practice, obstructed our growth. Church communities are arranged, by chance, to inhibit numerical growth. This is because the energy of everyone concerned is with the 'maintenance' of this group."

In many city-center churches the people have become walls to hold the community together. There is little energy to spare for mission and ministry. When the community meets for one hour per week and its priority is its own survival there is little time for other issues; in fact, many downtown churches engage professionals or outsiders to implement their ministries. The people become a ring of walls to hold the community together. These walls may also keep others out. This is analogous to the First Plan; a congregation surrounded by strong walls and engaged in contemplation: contemplation of the ministries they do not have the energy to pursue.

St. James' Piccadilly has been examining another model for a city center church: a network of small cells to supplement the Sunday congregation. The cells would take the church out into the world: each cell a little church. The members would worship together, eat together, study together and provide one another with mutual support. When the community does not have to expend its energy on keeping itself together, it is free to minister to others.

The Dome of Light is the realization of the Sixth Plan. In the world of nature the image of the Sixth Plan is the scattering of seeds, an analogy for the dispersal of a network of small cells, each of which is the church and each of which takes the light of the Eucharist out into the world. Thus the radical structure proposed for St. James' Piccadilly, which may be the way all downtown churches will look in the next century, is firmly founded on the Sixth Plan; the plan which supports the struggle for justice, peace and freedom for all.

# Chapter 11
# Supporting the Community

In the first four chapters of this book we learned how to configure space so it will support worship. In these final four chapters we will study what needs to be done to support the congregation in its worship. The needs of the congregation (which I listed in *"Theology for Atheists"*[69]) are:

1. The space must express welcome.

2. Everybody has to be able to see everything.

3. Everybody has to be able to hear and participate in what is sung and spoken.

4. The altar or communion table is to be the focus of the space.

5. Seating must be arranged to express "community", rather than "audience".

These are all essentials. I don't see how any church can dispense with any one of them, yet very few churches meet all these criteria. So why are we surprised to find that so many people are leaving?

**The people are leaving! What shall we do?**

In most churches attendance is down, and many are closing down altogether. It's the main item of concern for many discussion groups. Sometimes the true situation is disguised as "combining services" where one service replaces two, or as "merging congregations" where one church replaces two, but the fact is: membership is declining and churches are being closed at a great rate. Some church buildings are being recycled into community centers or replaced as condominiums, some are attempting to hang on to their past as museums, and some are slowly crumbling into ivy-clad ruins, a historic plaque celebrating their past glories.

---

68. Robinson, Theology for Atheists, 164.

## Supporting the Community

Congregations are trying many things in an attempt to fix the problem: parish picnics, men's groups, bible study, children's programs, book clubs, retreats, youth camps, film nights, yoga classes, pancake breakfasts, church suppers, video screens, choral concerts—none of it seems to be working. The one thing that receives no attention, and the one thing that only the church can offer, is worship. All the churches problems would be solved if worship became such an exciting engaging experience it would draw in the crowds; but it's not. In living memory it never has been! We can look back with nostalgia to the days when churches were filled to capacity and congregations were expanding, but I'm not sure there were any more real worshipers then than we have today. Most of the people who showed up for church in those golden years did so because there was nothing else to do on a Sunday. When I first came to Canada in the 1950's I arrived in Toronto on a Sunday and all the stores were closed. The local department stores had drapes drawn across their windows so passers-by would not be tempted from their devotions. Swings and teeter-totters in public parks were chained up so small children would not be distracted by these secular attractions. There was no Sunday shopping, you couldn't get a drink on a Sunday, no theatre or film shows, no alternative to going to church. It gave the phrase "being driven to church" a new meaning. It's what everybody did, the lowest common denominator.

Before we start to mourn the passing of a golden age of church attendance I think we should consider what was taking place in the church in those days. Most of those attending were not there for the worship, they were showing up as a result of social pressure or because on a Sunday there was nothing much else to do. We cannot look back and say that large attendances showed that worship was popular in those days; and that the liturgy had a perfection that we should attempt to emulate today. It was not perfect in those days, and the vast crowds that showed up were not attracted by the liturgy, they came to get out of the house, to get dressed up, and to meet and have conversations with friends. The true predominant religion at that time was not Christianity, it was "church-going".

In earlier times attendance was even more strictly enforced. In Calvin's church in Geneva one of the duties of the Deacon was to take attendance, and if a member did not show up on a Sunday the Deacon would visit his home on the Monday, and if the absentee did not have a sufficiently good excuse he would have to present himself at the church for judgment. In his "Ecclesiastical Ordinances of Geneva"[70] Calvin writes

> "If anyone is negligent in attending worship so a noticeable offense is evident for the communion of the faithful, or if anyone shows himself contemptuous of ecclesiastical discipline, he is to be admonished. If he becomes obedient he is to be dismissed in love. If he persists, passing from bad to worse, after having been admonished three times, he is to be excommunicated and denounced to the magistrate."

In a similar vein, when a student at my son's school informed the Headmaster that he should be excused from attending Chapel "because he did not believe in God", the Headmaster replied "The only thing you have to believe here is that attendance at Chapel is compulsory."

The main problem lies in the way most churches are arranged: they are set up so they do not support community. Yet Christians are required to worship in community: that is what Jesus demands of us. Worship is very different from private prayer. For worship we must be "gathered together". Imagine that you had been invited to a gathering and when you arrived everybody turned their back on you—how would that make you feel? Would this be the welcome you had been promised? Would you want to be part of such an unfriendly group, even if they were proclaiming their love for you? And yet that is the way almost all churches are arranged—when seated in the pews all you can see is the backs of other people's heads. If your church follows this pattern, with parallel pews facing the same way, its days are numbered. You are promised relief from this is alienation when you hear the words "The peace of the Lord be always with you!" At that point you are expected to stand up, turn round, and greet the people in the pew behind you, except that they have turned around too, so we are no further ahead.

The only way to arrange the seating so people will be able to see one another and have a sense of community is to have them sit in a ring, so they can see the faces of at least some of their brothers and sisters. This ring could be incomplete, as illustrated for the Second Plan, (figure 47, page 91) or a square ring as in St. Mark's Church in Burlington VT,

---

69. Calvin, Ordinances.

## Supporting the Community

(figure 37, page 77) but a ring nevertheless. I have found that every church I have ever worked with has needed this change. That is the way the worshipers gathered in the Early Church—the way the church was arranged in the first few centuries of its existence, and the rapid expansion of the church shows that this format served its congregations well. Nowadays most churches have adopted a different pattern for worship: one that was conceived for the Victorian age. This has a sentimental appeal for some people, but for most of us who live in a very different society we are not well served by what we have inherited. It's no small wonder that the church is in decline. We don't need all that religious clutter. Jesus' message was simple: he reduced 613 commandments to two, and he did not need clerical robes to preach in nor a chancel to preach from. We got "off track" when the church became a pillar of support for the establishment but that is now changing, so we need to revert back to an earlier model that will better serve us.

After a typical service visitors are invited "to join us for Coffee Hour". Sometimes we do not realize the importance of this ministry, and we have not taken full advantage of this opportunity for community building. We file down the stairs at the back of the church and enter the church basement. Windows set high in walls of painted concrete block proclaim that we are now underground. Here, under fluorescent lights we sit on folding chairs at collapsible tables while munching on chocolate-chip cookies and holding mugs of tea or coffee—beverages which are almost indistinguishable. A few brave souls are still wearing a sticker saying "Visitor"—the rest have fled.

Don't we deserve better than this? We would not patronize a café or coffee shop that offered such sub-standard facilities so why do we excuse them for a church? Why is there no espresso machine, no toaster oven, and so little comfort or charm? The cathedrals in Britain do it much better. Many of them offer a meal service in the crypt, its romantic setting offering an added enhancement, and this becomes a profit center for them.

I proposed a measure that would solve both of these problems for Trivitt Memorial Church in Exeter, a farming community in southern Ontario. The church was built for a congregation of 600, but with agribusiness replacing the farm family such a capacity is no longer needed, which made it possible to combine the community space with the worship space, eliminating the need for everybody to make a trek to the parish hall, and affirming the central value of community. The "back" rows of pews, fitted with carpet treads, can slide easily on the wood floor, and the deal was that if the teenagers in the congregation would quickly

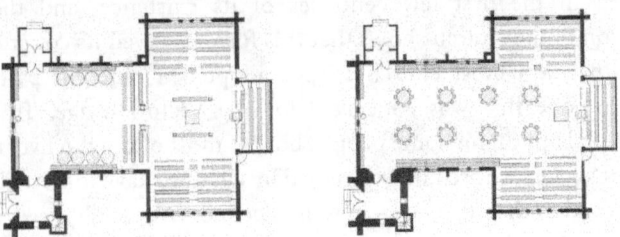

FIGURE 102. For Trivitt Memorial Church the back pews (as seen in the plan on the left) can be slid out of the way, freeing the whole space for an after-service Coffee Hour (as seen on the right).

move the pews to the sides after the service the church would play, over the church sound system, whatever music the movers requested as a substitute for the regular organ postlude.

There's a paradox which this illustrates: that pews are more flexible than chairs. If Trivitt Memorial church were fitted out with chairs instead of pews it would take ten times longer to move and replace the seating, and instead of being entertained by a single track of RadioHead the congregation would have had to endure the entire album.

**The Invitation**

For many people their first contact with a church will be by way of the internet, so the church website is of prime importance. It needs to be designed with sensitivity to the needs and mindset of the enquirer. We need to do this with great care because we will only get feedback from our successes—those whom we have failed we will never hear from again. Here are some points to bear in mind:

> 1. Never mention the word "Welcome!" Welcome is an expression of a warm personal relationship, it is not a slogan.
>
> 2. Have a vertical menu prominent on the first page. Do not rely on the fine print on a horizontal toolbar. This gives the enquirer the freedom to go directly to what he/she considers to

be most important, it does not impose somebody else's priorities.

3. Do not mention "our mission". High-flown phrases are seldom believed. Talk about "what you will find" rather than about "who we are".

4. Avoid "church-speak": the private language of the initiated. That goes for ecclesiastical titles too. In particular avoid titles like "The Venerable Canon the Rev'd Dr. So-and-so, BA, MDiv, DMin, Incumbent and Parish Priest" (but that does not mean that the priest has to appear in shirtsleeves.)

5. Avoid crosses and other religious symbols. The church is not a church for Christians, it's a church for seekers and sinners. When Jesus appointed the Twelve he did not enquire about their beliefs, he just said "Follow Me!"

6. Avoid having lots of photographs of happy smiling people like a family album. The church is also for the sad and the broken.

7. Have a page outlining the programs on offer, and

8. Have a page that lists all the practical stuff like service times, phone numbers, street address, available parking, access map, child care, etc. Some churches omit to mention the town in which they are located, expecting everyone to know.

9. If your church is "historic" it might be best to give a link to a separate site for the historical stuff, so your welcome to a new future is not overshadowed by the dead hand of the past.

The church should have a presence on the street. If the building is in reasonable repair it will be obvious that it is a church. It will not need any additional symbolism. A sign will be needed outside the church. This should be severely edited to bear just the needed information: the name of the church, its denomination, its e-mail address, and a listing of service times are all that is required. There is no need to record the priest's name, or to embellish the sign with some catchy slogans. And again, no mention of the word "Welcome", and no crosses.

## The Welcome

The principal entry to the church, the most prominent one, should be the one everybody uses, or at least it should be available to everybody. This is the way a stranger will attempt to enter, so a sign on the door saying "Please use side entrance" will give rise to frustration, and you don't get a second chance to make a first impression. This is particularly infuriating when the sign says "Disabled entrance at the rear". It is essential, no matter what, that everybody be entitled to use the same entrance. If this cannot be achieved the church should resort to dynamite, or close.

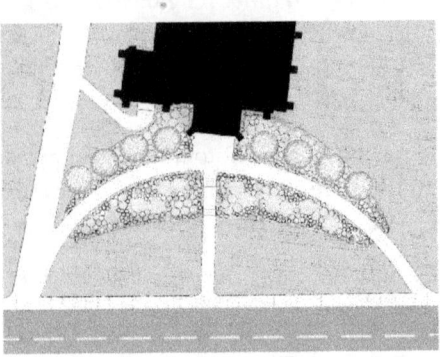

FIGURE 103. At the Church of St. Mary Magdalene in Picton the diagonal ramps are more direct for all pedestrians than the original formal walkway with steps.

Sometimes it has been found that making the main entrance accessible to the disabled benefits all worshipers. This was proposed for the Church of St. Mary Magdalene in Picton, Ontario (figure 103). Raising the level of the ground at the front of the church by a floral bank or berm would make it possible to install a pair of diagonal ramps for wheelchair access. This would provide a route that is more convenient for all pedestrians, as well as bypassing the original central steps whose role will become more ceremonial. If lack of space demands a serpentine route rather than a direct one this would still benefit those with baby carriages or walkers, and small children would enjoy the challenge of a winding path.

When a newcomer visits the church his first human contact will be with the Welcoming Guild. This would consist of a minimum of four people—two greeters and two ushers, all wearing name tags. They would stand at the sides of the entry way, leaving the center free. With a big smile one of the greeters would ask "Hello. Is this your first time here?" and hand him a service sheet, indicate where coats may be hung, and introduce him to one of the ushers. The usher will offer to make out a name tag which should be identical to all the others so it's not seen as a target. Then she takes the new arrival to a seat and perhaps sits with him for the service. The greeters and ushers have the most important job in the church. Their role is more vital than that of the preacher when it comes to the survival and growth of the community, yet few of us have natural abilities in this area. However, those skills can be learned and developed, and a serious program needs to be in place to teach and practice them—a form of amateur dramatics where we can rehearse role-playing.

Such service and devotion needs to be honored by the community, and members of the Welcoming Guild could wear medallions or ribbons as a token of that respect. Their role in essential to ensuring the survival of the church.

**Sacred Meeting**

Rudolf Schwarz's Second Plan gathers up all the measures we have discussed in this chapter. The Second Plan, Sacred Meeting, supports the ministry of Pastoral Care which will be the most vital ministry of the church in the next century. It is a ministry of deep personal involvement, which will set it against the trends that are developing in society. We are finding that expressions of relationship are becoming more superficial and objectified as the world goes digital. This purpose for the Second Plan is discussed in chapter 6. The other five Plans are more specialized in their application, but it is the worship associated with the Second Plan that will generate the energy for the church to branch out into the ministries related to those other Plans when needed; to create a light to shine out into the world.

The iconic illustration for the Second Plan (figure 47, page 91) illustrates the seating arrangement we have discussed in this chapter: a ring of seating that offers "free and unimpeded access between the People and the Sacraments." This is a close and direct contact where we experience the space, the Sacraments and one another with our physical bodies; a real close-ness not found in a virtual world.

To round-out the ministry of the church the Mandala (figure 25, page 46), which is based on the Cycle of Worship, demands that we adopt two secondary ministries. A trace illustrated on page 47 shows that for a congregation that has adopted Pastoral Care as its primary ministry, its secondary ministries should be Witness and Evangelism. Both of these ministries include "world" as one of their parameters, so by adopting these two secondary ministries the thrust of the congregation will be extended out into the world. In this chapter we have suggested measures that support these two ministries with precision. We have advocated that the church have a tangible presence, both on the Internet and on the street. These are invocations of the Ministry of Witness. The Ministry of Evangelism will be celebrated when we support the Welcoming Guild, those greeters and ushers that are our front-line troops in a campaign to grow the church. Using Rudolf Schwarz's gift of Sacred Meeting we can illuminate the world.

**Nobody Left Behind**

Rebuilding the Church, if not well handled, can divide the community it is to serve. If the church appoints a Building Committee and charges it with formulating a proposal for renewal and presenting it to the community . . . that venture is doomed to fail. Some members of the community will feel the proposal to be an elitist creation in which they have had no involvement, and many will reject the proposal for that reason alone. This was the situation in which I found myself, as a young architect, many years ago.

A local congregation had grown to the point that their church had become overcrowded, and the newly-appointed Building Committee asked me to prepare plans to illustrate the three options they had selected: knock out the front wall and build a new chancel, build a gallery at the back for the overflow, or knock the whole thing down and start again from scratch. I was asked to provide drawings of each option so the congregation would understand what they were getting into. On voting day the drawings were pinned up in the church, and one of the committee's options (I cannot remember which one) carried the day; but the losers became so angry that half the congregation left the church. This effectively solved the problem of overcrowding, but not in a way that had been anticipated!

As an attempt to avoid this situation another approach is to involve the whole community in the decision-making process. The church might engage a professional conciliator to lead discussions in a series of study sessions or workshops, perhaps with input from various visiting experts. This is the process recommended in *Re-pitching the Tent*,[71] published in 1996. It sounds good, but, unfortunately, I have never known this process to yield a satisfactory result. In these discussions we don't spend any time dealing with what we agree on. More and more we focus on what divides us, creating divisions where none existed before, which makes it hard to proceed with any change. When we have become exhausted by the process we adopt just that minimum that makes no real difference.

I had to confront this situation a few years ago when I was engaged as a Liturgical Consultant by the Church of St. John the Evangelist in Ottawa. This is an enthusiastic forward-looking church which has inherited a worship space with severe problems that cripple its worship. To deal with this, over the years the church had commissioned studies by architects and other consultants, five studies in total. When these proposals were put to the vote each one had been accepted by the congregation by a margin of approximately 65 percent. However, this margin was considered to be insufficient to allow any of the projects to proceed as 35 percent of the congregation had expressed dissatisfaction, so nothing was done.

I did not want to be responsible for a sixth failure, so I had to create a whole new approach. My proposal was that I would take sole responsibility for developing, in camera, a concept for the future of the church, and I would present this to the entire community at a special vestry meeting. Despite numerous offers of help I resolved that no member of the community would have any advanced notice of the proposal, not the priest, nor the administrator, and not any of the pillars of society.

When the day for the special vestry arrived there was an excitement in the air. By revealing the proposal to everybody at the same time it was like the unveiling of a work of art or a first-night at the theatre. And with two abstentions the proposal was accepted unanimously. This despite the

---

70. Giles, Re-pitching the Tent.

fact (or perhaps because of the fact) that the proposal was far more radical than any of the previous offerings. I have used this process with other communities, and never has the acceptance rate been less than 95 percent—a record unheard-of in the Anglican Church.

How was it possible to achieve this outcome?

First, in a PowerPoint presentation I explained to the community how their present church came to be the way it was, tracing out the development of church buildings from biblical times to the present day, and showing that their "traditional" format was a relatively recent development, perhaps an aberration, and for a developing world the church needs to adapt to a new future.

Then I walked the people through Rudolf Schwarz's relationships between space and worship which are outlined in the first four chapters of this book. From this we deduced that their primary ministry was Pastoral Care., and we studied the implications for this ministry.

To explain how these could be incorporated into their space I built a model of a new arrangement which is illustrated in figure 105 on page 203 in the next chapter. This shows the old pews reconstituted to form a ring around a central altar, with the outer rows banked so everybody gets a good view. The existing chancel is blocked-off, leaving just enough space for the choir stalls, with the organ above.

The remainder of the chancel, now separated from the church, becomes a small chapel, about 28 feet square, but with an impressive 40-foot ceiling height—what a wonderful space! Towering over the old high altar is the magnificent stained glass window which originally had the dignity of being the east window of the former church. In this chapel are gathered together all the memorabilia of the old church; the dedications and funerary plaques, the regimental flags, the wooden pulpit. the brass eagle, and a location is reserved for a columbarium to receive the ashes of our beloved dead. The new chapel offered a much more respectful venue for these heritage items than was available in the old church. One reason for the success of this project was because nothing was lost, and nobody was left behind. The proposal offered not an improvement to the church but a transformation; a new way of being church, and this promise of a new life was exciting and inspiring.

## Who can undertake this work?

A difficult question. Perhaps an architect, but not one who specializes in designing churches, or one who has a strong denominational affiliation. Perhaps an architectural or an engineering student, one with an independent mindset. Or a hands-on person who could follow the processes outlined in this book. Great genius or creativity is not required—just have a clear goal of what is to be achieved and be able to formulate this in a brief for your architect. What *is* required is to have a mind open to new ideas, the courage to dare to be different, and a willingness to serve. This will create a space where worship is supported, but that alone will not guarantee success. With the church rebuilt (on a new foundation) the worship of the people also needs to be led. This is the role of the priest or pastor, a role that is as important as the space itself. The role of the priest is similar to the role of a performer in creating beautiful music. Music is born with a composer, and to render it a performer is needed, and that performer needs an instrument. For congregational worship Schwarz is the composer, this book is the instrument, and with it the pastor can create beautiful harmonies to support, serve, and delight.

# Chapter 12
# Supporting the Sacrament of the Eucharist

**Moving the Furniture**

In the last chapter we agreed that the worshipers need to sit in a ring if they are to feel that they are a community rather than just an audience. It was also a requirement that the communion table should be the focus of the space, as a reflection of the central importance of the Eucharist to our faith. There can be little doubt that both of these requirements are necessary for the worshipers to feel that they are a worshiping community. Putting these two requirements together means that the communion table or altar needs to be at the center of the body of worshipers. In a "traditional" church this might be achieved by moving all the worshipers into the chancel if there is room for them; but more frequently it would require moving the altar into the body of the church.

This brings into question the need to have a chancel at all! Indeed the word "chancel" is derived from the Latin *cancellus*, meaning lattice or screen. These are devices for creating separations, for keeping people apart. They are barriers to the creation of community. How did we come to get these in the first place? Let's go back to the early church.

**The Early Church**

The first Christians would meet for Eucharist in one another's houses. Many of the letters to young churches contain such greetings as "Greet Priscilla and Aquila ... and the church that meets at their house." which opens the Letter to the Romans.

As numbers grew, larger spaces were required. Some public buildings such as basilicas were made available, rented, or taken over. Basilicas were built for the purpose of law courts. They had a single seat for the Prefect, sometimes set in a semicircular apse and a rectangular volume, sometimes with a double row of columns as in the first illustration of Figure 104. When used for Christian worship a communion table would be set in the center of the space. It is interesting that the basilica is now regarded as the traditional plan for the Roman Catholic Church; a heritage based on the form of real estate available for rental in second-century Rome.

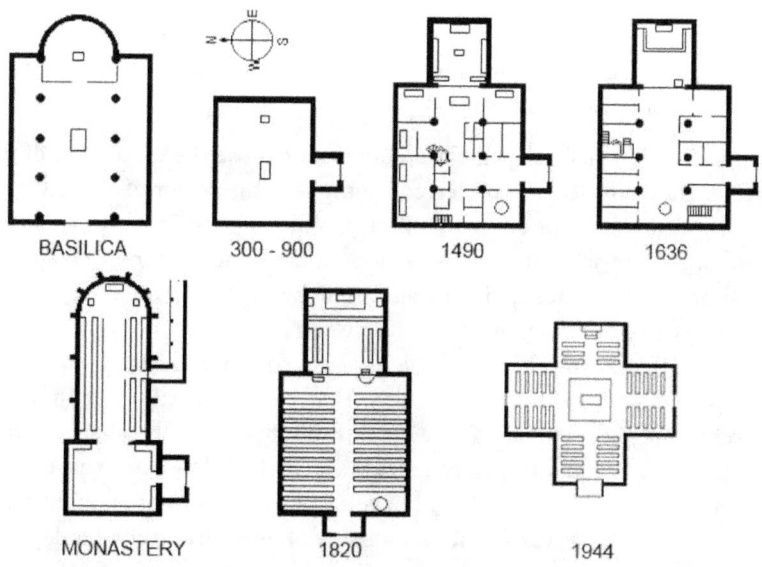

FIGURE 104. The development of the Christian Church.

When the community grew to the point where it could construct its own buildings these were in the form of a single room with a central altar and a seat for the presider. For many centuries this was the way churches were built.

In the Middle Ages multiple altars were introduced so that several masses could be held on the same day while respecting Catholic dogma that the mass was a sacrifice so it's altar could only be used once on any given day. The 1490 illustration shows a typical church with seven altars, which for a pilgrimage church would allow dedications to a total of seven saints, creating seven profit centers.

## Rebuilding the Church

At the Reformation Martin Luther repudiated these self-serving doctrines[72], saying: "Let us therefore repudiate everything that smacks of sacrifice, together with the entire canon, and retain only that which is pure and holy, and thus order our mass."

After the Reformation the Church of England returned, in the main, to a single altar, with options for its placement. The Book of Common Prayer of 1552 states:

> "The Table havyng at the Communion tyme a fayre white lynnen clothe upon it, shall stande in the body of the Churche, or in the chauncell."

Thus Cranmer left it open for a church to choose the placement of its table. He seems to have preferred having it in the center of the space as that was the first option he mentioned, and his life's work was to make worship more accessible to the people. At the same time John Hooper[73], Bishop of Gloucester said "The altar shall be made of wood, and not be so heavy that two men might not easily carry it."

In this he implied that the altar or communion table could be moveable, so it could be set where it is most needed. But in 1636 Archbishop Laud, wishing to augment the dignity of the altar and the status of its attendants, decreed that the altar should be at the east end of a separated chancel, and should have a railing or fence as an additional separation, and that is the situation many of us have inherited today.

### The Monastic Tradition

While all this was taking place monasteries were following a different path. Monks were required to gather for worship up to eight times a day for Matins, Lauds, Prime, Terce, Sext, None, Vespers and Compline. For this they assembled in the Choir, a room with facing choir stalls and an altar at the east end. The choir was not reserved for those monks with the best voices, all the monks were required to chant all the prayers. An open room was built on to the west end of the choir where the townspeople could come and observe the monks' devotions but there

---

71. Jasper, Prayers of the Eucharist, 144, 192.

72. Hooper, A Holy Confession

was no question of their being allowed to participate. Probably they would not have been able to anyway because the worship was all in Latin. The people did not worship in this situation, they were being allowed to witness the worship of others.

## The Modern Church

It was in the 1820's that the Cambridge Camden Society, a group of intellectuals and aesthetes at Cambridge University, sought to recover an ancient piety by resurrecting an ancient form of church building. They could have chosen the form of the early Christian churches, a single space where the people gather around a central table, but it was unfortunate that they opted for something much more theatrical. They chose to follow the monastic model. True, it was ancient, but in that particular set-up the people had very little involvement in the worship.

It was this arrangement that morphed into the plan for what we now call the traditional church; and virtually all churches built after 1820 adopted this plan. A shortened monk's choir becomes the new chancel which retains the same inward-facing seating plan for its choir of singers. At the same time the nave expands and lengthens to accommodate larger crowds. The plan also perpetuates another tradition: it does little to encourage participation by the people. They sit on wooden benches arranged in parallel rows on a flat floor, and through an archway they can see (or rather, those in the front few rows can see, the rest can see only the backs of people's heads) a raised chancel where a robed choir occupies inward facing stalls, and beyond that, up still more steps and behind a fence an altar is set against the end wall. The chancel would be brightly lit, in fact one of the requirements of the Cambridge Camden Society was that the lighting in the nave should be kept dim[74] to enhance the feeling of being present at a sacred mystery.

Virtually all churches that have been built after that time have followed such a plan. It has come to be regarded as "traditional", although as a tradition it is very recent. Before 1820 you would find it hard to discover any church anywhere which followed this so-called traditional plan. That plan persists as the norm to the present day, featuring a raised chancel, a remote altar, a flat floor, and a central aisle

---

73. Brine, *The Camden* Society, vol 2, no 1.

with parallel rows of pews to accommodate the shrinking congregation. The long central aisle does not make these churches examples of Sacred Journey. Their rigid arrangement of pews holds the worshipers in an iron grip which prevents them from journeying anywhere. In contrast, the two churches illustrated in chapter 8: the chapels at Gethsemeni Abbey and Trinity College, allow the worshipers to leave their seating area and make the journey into a spacious chancel where they gather into a more informal assembly surrounding an altar where the sacrament is brought to them. One should not have to line up in a queue for Holy Communion. A church is not a cafeteria. Grace is a gift, not a ration.

An exception to the traditional format was so notable it found itself recorded in TIME magazine. In 1944 St. Mark's Church in Burlington, Vermont, adopted a central altar with a surrounding congregation (see page 77). We can see, at last, some signs that the old order is changing.

**Seating for Seeing (and Seeing is Believing)**

If you have a flat floor the people in the front row can see just fine, and if the seating is with chairs these can be arranged so the second row chairs are centered on the gaps between those of the front row. However the view from the third row is obstructed by the people in front. Pews come off better, because you can always slide yourself a bit to the right or a bit to the left, so the front three rows of pews can have a good view. Beyond this, the seating needs to be raised if the people are going to be able to see. This is achieved in even the most humble hockey arena in rural Ontario, where it is a given that everybody should be able to see all the ice, so why would anybody wish to put up with the sub-standard conditions that are found in a church?

Raised seating is not difficult to accomplish. It does not require a lot of heavy construction, just some simple platforms that can sit on the existing floor in a series of six-inch steps. These can be built by a local carpenter, or as a work project by members of the community. I have recommended this for almost every church that has engaged me as a consultant. You can see an example in the last three rows of pews in the transepts of Trivitt Memorial Church (figure 102, page 190). The model for the Church of St. John the Evangelist in Ottawa (figure 105) is a typical example of this form of seating. Notice how raising just a few rows of pews alters the whole feel of the space, transforming a classroom into an amphitheater, and implying that something really important is happening in the center.

FIGURE 105. A model of the Church of St. John the Evangelist in Ottawa, showing the drama that is possible when stepped pews create an amphitheater.

Raised seating also makes the back rows of seating part of the community, so those who choose to hide at the back in order to be safe can still participate.

## Let there be Light

This is a warning. If, as an experiment, you attempt to move the altar into the center of the space "to see if people will like it" without first adjusting the lighting, the experiment will fail. People won't like it. They will still have a brightly lit and highly decorative chancel from which the altar has been moved into a strangely unfamiliar position. It will seem odd. To allow the altar to be the focus of a new space it also has to be the focus of new lighting. It has to be the brightest object in the room.

Theatrical spotlights, such as the ETC Source-Four units, will be needed for this because the beams need to be carefully controlled so they don't shine in people's eyes. At least four units will be needed for a typical installation, shining in from the four corners. These lamps can sometimes be purchased "used", or for an experimental installation they can be rented from a theatrical supply house.

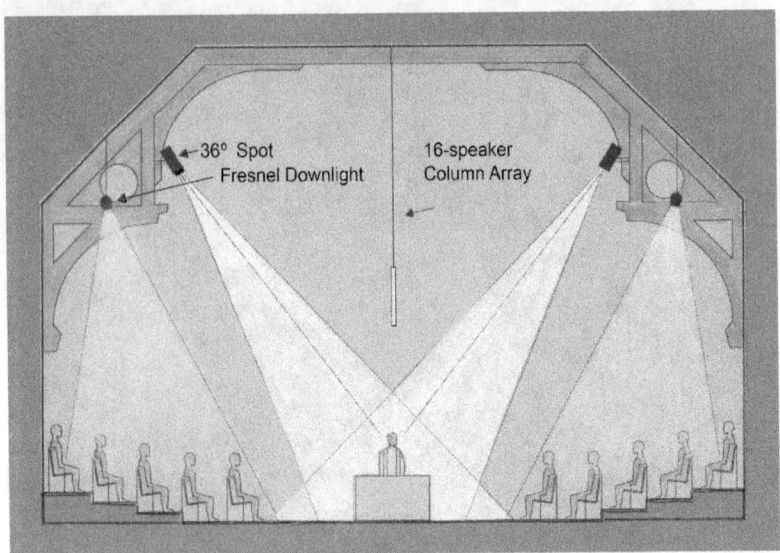

FIGURE 106. Lighting pattern for a central focus.

The lamps should be placed so the light falls on the head of the presider at 45°. If the beams are more vertical the presider's eyes will be in deep shadow creating what is known as "raccoon eyes" and it will not be possible to see any facial expressions; and if the beams are more horizontal they will shine in the presider's eyes. How to create a 45° beam? It's easy! Take a sheet of paper and fold it so two adjacent edges come together. This will make an angle of 45°. Now stand where the presider will stand and, holding an edge of the paper horizontal, sight along the sloping edge. That will tell you where the electrician should hang the lights. And notice in the illustration how adjustable baffles (known as barn doors) on the fixture allow the beam to be trimmed so the upper edge just avoids lighting up the people in the front row. This will give a wonderful focus on what is important.

## The Invitation that Isn't

Finally, a note on what might appear to be an invitation but is in fact as exclusion. Many Anglican and Episcopal churches have a note on the service sheet or an exhortation from the pulpit saying:

> "All baptized Christians are welcome to receive the consecrated bread and wine at this service."

Fifty years ago this would have been a statement of ecumenism, welcoming the Catholics, the various Orthodox, and Presbyterians, to join with Anglicans in worship. But what about those who are still seeking a faith, or are getting by without one? Do we not wish these to feel welcome? This is handled well at the Church of St. George the Martyr in Toronto. Printed in the service sheet is the message:

> "Throughout the history of Christianity the communion meal has been shared by baptized members of the Christian family. If you love Jesus, or if you want to love Jesus, or if you want to want to love Jesus, we invite you to share in this meal together."

When Jim Fisk was Rector of The Church of the Holy Trinity in Toronto he said "Anyone who walks in through the door of this church is a member of this church"; and that included me. If anyone had demanded that I had to acknowledge my disowned proxy-baptism before I would be allowed to participate in the life of the community I would have walked out again.

Originally Jim had cookies and a flask of orange juice on the Table so the kids could participate too. When the ecclesiastical authorities pointed out to him that this was a gross misreading of scripture we figured that a little bit of wine would not do the kids any harm

# Chapter 13

# Supporting the Sacrament of the Word

**Praise the Lord! Praise His Holy Name!**

Although not usually included in a listing of the sacraments, there can be little doubt that scripture is a channel by which God's grace is imparted to us. It offers us insights into spiritual truths, guides our behavior, offers us forgiveness, inspiration and hope. One cannot imagine a church without it.

Many sermons begin with the preamble "May nothing but truth be spoken here, and nothing but truth be heard". In some churches this is difficult. The acoustics are so muffled that it is hard to hear anything, while in others there is so much echo that what is spoken gets lost in the confusion. How bad is the echo? A room's sound quality is judged by its reverberation time, the time it takes for sound to die away.

What is the ideal reverberation time? It depends on the event. I have listed in Figure 107 a series of recommendations for reverberation times for a variety of performances. The first item, "speech-lecture", gives a range of about half-a-second to one-and-a-half seconds as ideal for a lecture where clarity is most important for the accurate delivery of information. I have created a new category "speech-church" because speeches given in church have a more ceremonial quality which goes beyond merely imparting information. One speaks slower in church, as if the words were more important—perhaps they are! For this I recommend a range of 1.0 to 2.5 seconds.

For music there are four categories listed. For chamber music where precision is important a range of 1.0 to 1.5 seconds is preferred, while for orchestral music a range of 1.3 to 2.6 seconds would be fine. Choral music is a compromise because we want to experience the blend of voices, but we also want to understand the words, so a range of 1.6 to 2.8 seconds will support both the choir and congregational singing. Finally, for the organ an ideal range starts at 2.5 seconds and extends to

4.5 seconds, although many organists would find this range inadequate and would like the range to extend even further, perhaps to 5 or 6 seconds, although that would limit the use of the space for anything else but organ recitals. The sweet spot where all these uses come together is at 2.4 seconds, an acoustic that works for preacher, choir, congregation and organ,

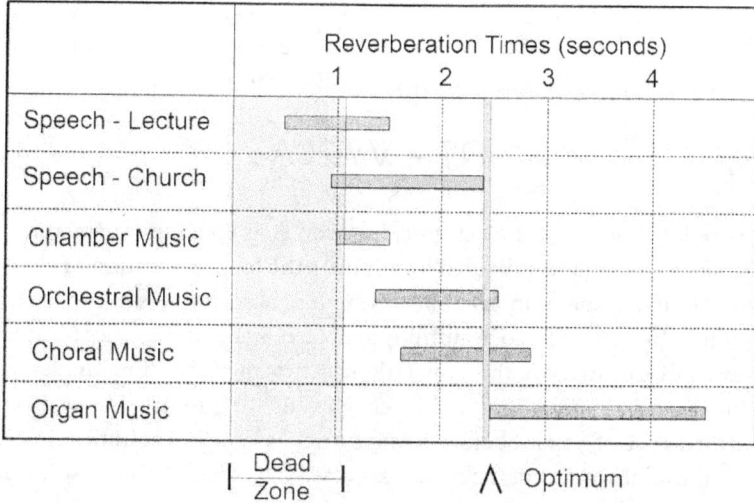

FIGURE 107. Recommended Reverberation Times for various performances,

One other observation: if the reverberation time is less than 1.1 seconds the sound will die away faster than the human ear can follow it, so the space will appear to have no reverberation at all! This is the dead zone, where there is no perceptible echo. This is the situation in those large evangelical churches where the Praise Choir is equipped with microphones and an artificial reverberation is added to their voices electronically. This does nothing for the rest of us. Under these circumstances it's really hard for the congregation to participate in making a joyful sound before the Lord because their voices don't sound like they are contributing anything.

Up to the beginning of the twentieth century the only way to predict the acoustic response of a new space was by copying an existing one. Thus the beautiful response of the Musikverein in Vienna was achieved by copying the "shoebox" form of the Leipzig Gewandhaus, and this was again copied for the new Symphony Hall in Boston. However, when Harvard University built its new Fogg Lecture Hall in 1895 the acoustics were so terrible lectures were impossible. Something had to be done. The University asked a young physics professor, Wallace Clement Sabine, to investigate the situation. Armed with a stop-watch and an organ pipe Sabine spent the next few years investigating reverberation times for different facilities. He discovered that the size of the space and the materials of which it is constructed are the factors which influence reverberation times. The bigger the space the more reverberation, while absorbent materials reduce it. He established the formula

$$RT = V / 20A$$

where RT, the reverberation time, in seconds, is equal to the volume of the space in cubic feet divided by 20 times the total absorption of all the surfaces in the space. In his honor the unit of absorption is known as the "sabin". This formula, so beautifully simple, matches in elegance Sir Isaac Newton's formula for the gravitational attraction of falling apples, or Einstein's famous $e = mc^2$. It enables us to predict the acoustic performance of a space before a single brick is laid. The volume referred to is the total volume of the space expressed in cubic feet. The absorption is obtained by multiplying the area of each exposed surface by the absorption coefficient for its material and totaling them. To demonstrate this process I have applied it to the Church of St. Mary Magdalene in Picton as an example. Picton is a small Ontario town with a population of 5,000. The church, built in 1913, has a disappointing, dull, muffled acoustic. Let's find out why, and what can be done about it.

First we have to calculate the volume of the church, which is the floor area multiplied by the average ceiling height. We don't have to be super-accurate about this—just pacing-off the floor dimensions to make a sketch plan and estimating the ceiling heights will be good enough. With a floor area of 4,095 square feet, and an average height of 29 feet, the total volume of the space is 118,800 cubic feet.

Calculating the acoustic absorption looks more complicated, but actually it is quite simple. In fact all my students have been able to calculate the reverberation times for their own churches by following this process, which is tabulated in Figure 108. This exercise is empowering; not only will it give you a value for the reverberation time of your own church, it will also identify those elements affecting it, and can indicate what adjustments will improve the situation. To assist you in doing this calculation for your own church I have inserted a blank table in Appendix B at the back of the book which you can photocopy, or if you wish you could enter your data into a spreadsheet program such as Excel which will do the calculations for you.

First, in Column A, list all the objects and exposed surfaces in the room. In Columns B and C list the dimensions of their surfaces. Multiply these to get the areas of surfaces for Column D. You can ignore doors and windows, just assume they are part of the wall. Notice that for some items, like pews, we list the floor area taken up by a block of pews in addition to the floor beneath them. In Column E we list the various materials of these items, and in Column F we list the absorption coefficients for those materials. Absorption coefficients for hundreds of materials and furnishings are listed on the internet. I have listed some of the more common ones in Appendix C. Most of these tables give values for a range of frequencies, but for our purposes we don't need super accuracy—we only need to be concerned with the coefficients in the 500Hz column (which corresponds to middle-C on a piano) as this is a good average. Multiply the area in Column D by the coefficient in Column F to give us the absorption for each element in Column G.

Two additional points:

- Air has an absorption of 0.5 sabins per thousand cubic feet of volume (the volume we have already calculated), so we can add this in, and

- People have an absorption of 4 sabins per person, so this too we can add in to see the effects of our present and future congregations.

By totaling the entries in Column G we get a total absorption, A, which we can plug into the Sabine Formula to give us the Reverberation Time for the space. We see that for the Church of St. Mary Magdalene the reverberation time is 1.17 seconds, and Figure 107 tells us that such a low value puts the acoustic response of the church into the "dead zone", which is why the sound is so disappointing.

## Calculations of Reverberation Time
Floor Area 4,095 square feet, Average Height 29 feet,
Volume 118,800 cubic feet

| A<br>Element | B<br>Length (feet) | C<br>Width (feet) | D = BxC<br>Area | E<br>Material | F<br>Coeff @ 500 Hz | G = DxF<br>Absorption (sabins) |
|---|---|---|---|---|---|---|
| Walls (sides) | 205 | 20 | 4,100 | plaster | 0.02 | 82 |
| Walls (ends) | 88 | 30 | 2,640 | plaster | 0.02 | 52 |
| Openings | 14 | 5 | 70 | | 0.07 | 5 |
| | | | | | | |
| Floor | 24 | 35 | 840 | carpet | 0.39 | 327 |
| Floor | 44 | 74 | 3,256 | wood | 0.10 | 325 |
| | | | | | | |
| Ceiling | 105 | 54 | 5,670 | acoustic tile | 0.65 | 3,685 |
| | | | | | | |
| Pews | 27 | 17 | | seating | 0.10 | 46 |
| Organ Case | 10 | 13 | 130 | wood | 0.07 | 9 |
| People | | | | 120 people | 4.00 | 480 |
| | | | | | | |
| Air 118,800 ft³ | | | | | 0.5/1000 | 59 |
| | | | | | | |
| **Total Absorption** | | | | | | **5,070** |

**Reverberation Time**   118,800 / 20 x 5,070   = 1.17 seconds

FIGURE 108. Calculations for the existing Reverberation Time of the Church of St. Mary Magdalene, Picton, Ontario.

## Supporting the Word

Why is the sound in the church of St. Mary Magdalene so muffled? Let's do a bit of detective work. When we look at Column G we see that by far the biggest absorber is the acoustic tile on the ceiling, which accounts for 3,685 sabins. But in 1913 when the church was built acoustic tile had not yet been invented. The original ceiling would have been plaster like the walls, with a coefficient of 0.02 as opposed to 0.65 for acoustic tile (thus tile absorbs more than thirty times as much sound as plaster). Without the acoustic tile the plaster ceiling would have an absorption of 113 sabins instead of 3,685, giving a total absorption of 1,498 sabins for the original church. Plugging this value into the Sabine Formula gives us a reverberation time of 4.00 seconds. The table in Figure 107 tells us such an echoing space in the original church would delight the organist but be impossible for everyone else.

After a number of years an enterprising salesman convinced the church that their echo problems could be solved by gluing a brand new material called acoustic tile to the ceiling. In his enthusiasm he sold the church twice as much product as they needed, and the church went from too-noisy to too-dull, which is the way it is now.

What to be done? One solution might be to peel off half the tiles, but that might be messy. Another option could be to screw gypsum wallboard (drywall) to the ceiling to cover some of the tile. Gypsum wallboard is much softer and more absorbent than plaster. Its absorption coefficient is 0.07, compared with 0.02 for plaster. Covering just the acoustic tile of the sloping side panels of the ceiling with gypsum wallboard while leaving it in place for the flat center section would reduce the total absorption to 2,639 sabins. This would create a near-perfect reverberation time of 2.25 seconds for the church. Let's do it!

### Sing unto the Lord a New Song

Wallace Sabine has given us the tools we need to ensure that our voices will be heard. How can we assist those creating the sound—the readers, the choir, the congregation, and the organist?

### Support for the Preacher

In many churches the laity is taking on an increased role. They have not been trained as orators, so in most cases they will need a microphone.

In that case, the people are not listening to a speaker, they are listening to a loudspeaker. If this loudspeaker is not located close to the speaker there will be a split in perception. The sound will be seen as coming from one place but heard as if coming from another. This disassociation negates the immediacy of being in the same space as the speaker; one might as well just listen to a tape. Some people attempt to counteract this by mounting a pair of loudspeakers on either side of the chancel arch as if it were a stereo, in the hope that the sound might be heard as if coming from the center. This never works. Always, you hear only the sound from the loudspeaker that is closer to you. The only point at which these two sounds will merge is the on the centerline of the church, and usually this is the aisle where nobody sits. Particularly bad is the set-up where there is a row of tiny loudspeakers distributed along the side walls of the church. You may be inspired to see the preacher boldly declaiming something, but all you hear is a confidential whisper in your ear.

FIGURE 109. Cognitive disassociation: what you hear is not what you see.

We should also consider what sort of loudspeaker is needed. Some loudspeakers will just make the echo louder, with no net gain in clarity. For this situation a column speaker is ideal. I know it's counter-intuitive, but a vertical stack of speakers will cause the sound to be emitted in a horizontal band. Such a speaker array is shown in Figure 106 on page 204. It can be quite compact. The model shown is about 3 feet tall but only 2 inches square in size, and contains sixteen tiny speakers. The sound from this device will focus all the sound on the people, and it has considerable range. It will not cause confusing echoes to bounce down from the upper parts of the church because the narrow band of sound will never reach up that far.

However, all this raises the question of whether preaching belongs in a service of worship at all! The message might be interesting, but is this worship?

Preaching requires a silent community that is passively listening to wisdom dispensed from a raised chancel, or from an even-more-raised pulpit—a posture described as being "six feet above contradiction". It is an arrangement designed to inhibit interruption. Such a set-up could have been useful in ancient times when few people could read and bibles were rare, but now it is an outmoded inheritance. It is so unfortunate that we continue to propagate this unfunctional model: parallel pews on a flat floor and a raised chancel, after its need has passed.

We are required to worship in community, but by inhibiting the formation of community this top-down arrangement disrupts worship. Liturgy is "the work of the people", so worship demands the people's active role. It is ironic that the formation regarded as "traditional" is not even a good plan for learning about the bible. However when the people are sitting in a ring where they can discuss an introductory text or sermon the bonds of community are strengthened, and this can be a contribution to worship. It's time for a change.

## Support for the Choir

It's important for the choir to achieve a blend of sound, and for this they have to be able to hear one another as if they were one. The human ear cannot detect a sound delay of less than 20 milliseconds, and as sound travels at 1,000 feet per second this means the members of the choir should be within 20 feet of one another if they wish to hear themselves as a group. Also they would benefit by having a reflecting surface to augment their sound—the "bathroom effect". Such a surface should be within 10 feet of the singers so the there-and-back distance for the sound to travel will be less than 20 feet, and the singers will feel united. The old church builders knew this. In medieval cathedrals the choir stalls would be backed by a tall wooden partition to reflect the sound back to the choir, and sometimes the top would arch over the singers to increase the effect.

Should the choir be robed? That brings up the question "Are the choir performers or worshipers?" When a choir is singing from the chancel in a church of traditional layout it is clear that they are performers, so they should be robed like all the other occupants of that elevated space. However when a church has moved the altar out of the chancel, and perhaps has got rid of the chancel altogether, the choir has options. With the congregation surrounding the altar the choir can occupy the fourth side of the square, as illustrated by St. Mark's Church in Burlington VT (figure 37, page 77) and Trivitt Memorial Church (figure 102, page 190). If the primary purpose of the choir is to lead congregational singing, and perhaps offer a motet as background music when everybody else is receiving communion, then the choir are clearly worshipers and could wear the same street clothes as everybody else. However if the choir is performing an anthem as part of the music repertoire of the service they should have a uniform dress-style. When a group of singers is attempting to create a unified musical harmony it is distracting to be confronted visually by a variety of individual fashion statements. "Look, her slip is showing!" "Where did he get that sweater?" A test could be . . . "If everybody is sitting when the choir stands to sing, the choir should be dressed to have a uniform appearance!"

This does not mean the choir has to take on the implied sanctity of ecclesiastical garb. This is well handled at London's Church of the Annunciation Marble Arch. In this church, before the service begins, members of the choir quietly take their places. They wear black academic gowns over their street clothes, and I know from experience that academic gowns do not necessarily confer sanctity. In "The Parson's Handbook" of 1907 Percy Dearmer writes:

> "Properly, the choir should go quietly to their places when they arrive, and occupy the time before the service with prayer and recollectedness in the stalls instead of chatting in the vestry. If, however, they go in all together in processional order, no hymn should be sung, nor should there be any special hymn to accompany their return; and above all no cross should be carried."

In an ancient church, one with a long nave, a procession might have been the only way for the people at the back to see the priest; they would see him as he walked by; but with amphitheater-style seating everybody can see everything. A processional entry of a hymn-singing choir separates choir members from their community, and, if the procession carries a cross, signifying the holiness of the group, that tells us that Christ is not always present in his church.

**Support for the Congregation**

We have dealt, so far, with the way the congregation experiences the spectacles and sounds of worship, but a congregation also has an active role in worship. They recite the prayers and responses, chant the psalms and sing the hymns. They should be allowed to do this with a minimum of paperwork. In some churches they would be burdened with a prayer book, hymnbook, psalter, service sheet, parish bulletin, and an envelope. All that is required is that the service sheet should contain everything necessary for the service, with the exception of the hymn books which are already in the pews. They do this rather well at St. Matthias Church in Toronto—all the readings, prayers, and psalms for the service are presented in small three-ring leatherette binders where the contents can be changed week by week, yet they have more gravitas than a fistful of computer printouts. Included in the text are the rubrics "Now we stand", "Now we kneel", "Now we sit"; so everybody knows what is expected of them.

The congregation too is expected to sing. St. Augustine said "He who sings prays twice!" For singing to be a rewarding experience a good acoustic environment is essential—we are all opera stars in the shower. The requirements for enthusiastic congregational singing are exactly the same as those for the choir—an adequate reverberation time and a reflecting surface within ten feet. Without this one cannot hear the sound of one's own voice. It is as if the sound disappears as soon as it leaves the mouth, giving rise to feelings of "Why bother?" This is another great advantage of the amphitheater style of seating: the banked seating backs up against the sidewalls so four rows of seats are within ten feet of a reflecting surface, enabling a congregation to sing mightily.

## Support for the Organist

For several centuries the organ has been the traditional instrument to accompany choral singing. It is ideally suited for this role because it creates sound in the same way as the human voice—both generate sound from a vibrating column of air. This ensures a good blend. The same cannot be said for electronic organs. Here sound is generated by jerking a plastic cone back and forth. It's hard to describe the difference this makes, although the difference is very real. The best I can do is to observe that the sounds generated from pipes have an expansive quality while what emanates from a cabinet containing a loudspeaker sounds somehow throttled. I can always tell the difference, even when an electronic organ is broadcasting a sample set of sounds recorded from a famous pipe organ. Of course the initial investment for an electronic organ is much less than that for a small pipe organ, but the electronic organ may become obsolete or unrepairable in twenty years while a small pipe organ could last for centuries. Here are my recommendations, which go contrary to conventional wisdom:

> 1. For a really splendid performance instrument that will also support a choir install a large hybrid-electronic organ with three or more manuals, one of which is connected to a selection of pipes to accompany the singers.

> 2. If budget considerations do not allow this, install a medium-sized pipe organ, primarily to accompany choral singing.

> 3. If this is not possible, install a small portativ organ with a single manual and perhaps three ranks of pipes. This will not be a concert instrument, but will serve well to accompany a small choir.

> 4. If lack of funds will not allow that option, use a piano and save up for a portativ organ. An electronic organ such as is found in the chapels of funeral homes is not an option.

# Chapter 14
# Supporting the Sacrament of Baptism

**A Rite of Passage**

For almost two thousand years baptism has been the rite of entry to Christ's church. Most of the ceremonies taking place since that time were infant baptisms—parents would like to have their kids baptized so they could join and be with them as members of the community. For Roman Catholics there was an additional incentive. Catholic dogma stated that only the souls of the baptized could enter Heaven. If a little one happened to die before he had been baptized the best that could be done for him was to consign his soul to Limbo; that is the *Limbus Infantium*, a sort of daycare center in the sky where he would be well cared for but never be permitted to enter the glory of Heaven.

Baptism was a pre-condition for those wishing to be members of Christ's church. But for those wishing to take Holy Communion there was an additional hurdle: Confirmation. One had to take on personally those vows which had been made on the candidate's behalf by parents and godparents. I always resented the fact that I had been enrolled in a religion when I was too young to have any say in the matter—a forced conversion. However I retreated from that principled stand when I accepted Confirmation at the hands of the Bishop of St. Albans. At our school there was a rush to be confirmed as soon as possible and I was one of those rushing. Confirmation entitled one to attend the Holy Communion service at 8:30 am. It was all over by 9 o'clock and we would have the rest of the day free. Those boys who had not made that transition had to attend the 10:30 am Service of Morning Prayer which lasted for at least an hour-and-a-half, and included a lengthy homily by the Headmaster. In those days the transition was:

"Baptism, to Community, to Confirmation, to Communion."

That is all changing now. People are leaving the church in great numbers, and most of those leaving are baptized Christians. It is interesting that the rate of decrease in church membership in Canada is almost the same as the rise of Atheism—24 percent, although I would not wish to draw a connection between the two. Atheism is America's fastest-growing religion. A poll by Ipsos-Reid indicates that 28 per cent of those claiming to be Protestants "do not believe in God", and for Catholics the rate is 32 per cent. Essentially, these are atheists who wish to remain in the church, and in these groups there is not the same incentive for infant baptism—"we'll let her decide for herself when the time comes." For many, baptism is not seen as a requirement for belonging to a church community, and because the Eucharist stands at the heart of that community many do not require baptism as a pre-condition for partaking of Holy Communion, which is seen as a symbolic community meal. In recent times we have seen similar reversals. It used to be that marriage was the pre-condition for living-together, but the reverse seems to be normal today.

In some churches all are welcome at the table. Baptism then takes on a more serious role, a ceremony where adults may take up the cross, where they may take on the responsibility to affirm membership in Christ's church in an act of sacrifice, humility and joy. The former transition is being reversed. It is seen as:

"Communion, to Community, to Baptism"

Holy Communion is seen as a shared meal, an invitation to a relationship which over time will become deeper. As a culmination of this some will seek baptism to make a personal affirmation and commitment. Thus the ceremony of adult baptism will become much more meaningful than infant baptism where all the participants are surrogates.

**Celebrating the Sacrament**

The church must offer a welcome to all who enter. The community must be open to all. However some newcomers, wishing to celebrate their membership in the community, might seek to have that formalized by baptism. Up to now, infant baptism seems to have been the norm, but the signs are that this is changing. Increasingly baptism is becoming a matter of choice for adults rather than an imposition upon infants. No longer is infant baptism seen as a routine, a social vaccination for the very young. However for most churches the set-up for baptism remains infantile. The font, like a stone bird-bath, holds just a small quantity of water, and an even smaller quantity is delivered to the recipient by the agency of a moist thumb. This is such a poor symbol for the descending of the Holy Spirit from the Heavens in what should be a life-changing experience. The font holds a small quantity of water at changing-table height, a set-up that is convenient for bathing (or baptizing) babies but awkward for anything else.

To serve adult baptism where should the font be placed? There are three options...

- at the entrance to the church,

- in the heart of the community, and

- in a separate baptistery.

The separate baptistery should be a non-starter. It sets the font in a small room or alcove. It dates from the days when infant baptism was the norm and only parents and godparents would attend—a private family affair. And for baptizing an adult even more privacy was required. In the past there was something almost shameful about adult baptism, as if the candidate had missed out on something as a child and we now had to correct that situation later in life. When T. S. Eliot was baptized as an adult the ceremony took place at night, in a locked church, with just two witnesses present, and later the page was torn out of the parish register.

In the early church the font was set at the rear of the church, close to the entrance, to symbolize our entry into the faith. Several examples of this location can be seen in the plans of the churches in Figure 104, page 199. However in the 1950's baptism began to be regarded as the ceremonial rite of entry to the community, and it took place as part of the regular Sunday service. At this service it was awkward to have the font at the back of the church because everybody would have to turn their heads to see what was going on behind them. Some churches brought the font forward to the front of the church. This worked fine for a baptism, but the font was in the way for everything else, a permanent obstruction. I find it hard to accept one churches solution—they mounted their font on castors and wheeled it to wherever it would be needed. In this they effectively destroyed the symbolism of the font: its stone and water are to remind us of Christ's baptism in the River Jordan, and a river-on-wheels is a strange concept.

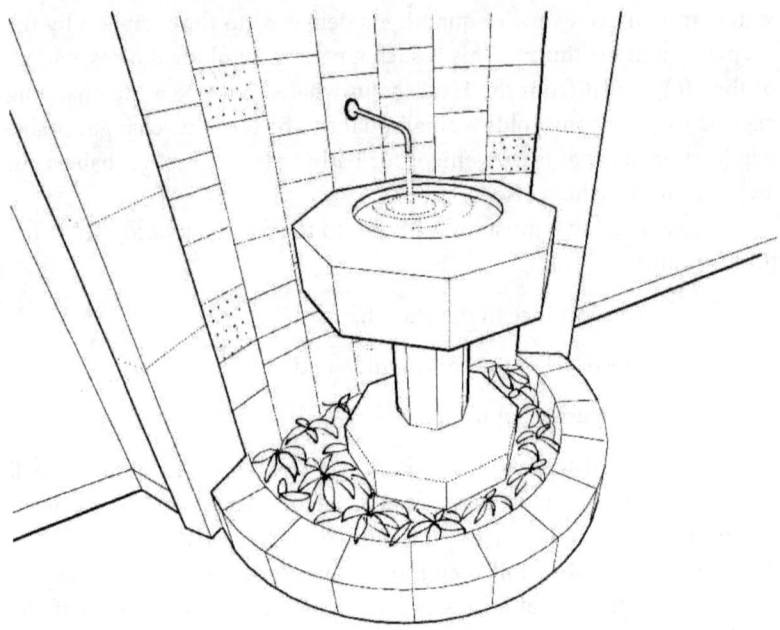

FIGURE 110. Living Water. The font proposed for St. John's Kanata.

What to do to make adult baptism a meaningful experience? . . . and remember Jesus was thirty years old when he was baptized. I am grateful to Kenneth Stevenson[75] for providing the seed of an idea, which is to separate the two functions of the font: the functions of being a source for the water of baptism and a venue for the ceremony. That was the basis of the proposal I made for St. John's Anglican Church in Kanata, Ontario. Here's how it would work:

The font is set near the entrance to the church, or in the narthex, in accord with ancient tradition. It has a water-line connection, so it is always full of water which, like grace, is allowed to overflow on to a pool or a planting bed, from which it is pumped back up to the font. This

---

74. Stevenson, The Mystery of Baptism, 154.

overflow is truly Living Water, nourishing the planting at its base and sweetening the air.

**The Ceremony**

The Baptism, however, would take place in the body of the church, at the heart of the community. Here something like a kids' plastic paddling pool is set up, with perhaps a sheet covering the cartoon characters.

A procession carrying three ewers of warm water makes its way through the church to the narthex, to the font. Here a small dipper of water from the font is added to each ewer, a homeopathic sanctification. The procession then returns to the body of the church for the Thanksgiving over the Water,

The candidate, wearing a white christening robe, kneels on a pad in the center of the pool where the three ewers of warm water are poured over him with the appropriate invocations. Then, soaking wet, the candidate rises up and is wrapped in a voluminous warmed terry-cloth robe of red, blue, green and gold, a coat of many colors, and holding a candle is anointed and greeted by the entire congregation. This is a meaningful celebration, full of deep symbolism, which can be adjusted to incorporate the wishes of the candidate.

**Envoi**

It is fitting that we should be ending this study of space and worship with a consideration of baptism: a new beginning. Adult baptism will be the token by which we can be confident that by shaping our spaces, ordering our worship, and welcoming the stranger we are assuring the survival of God's church in God's world. When adult baptism becomes the norm we will realize that once again our beloved church has returned to its first-century roots, to emerge once again as new.

*May it be so.*

*Amen.*

# Photo Credits

1. Henry Regnery Company, *The Church Incarnate*, 1958.

7. Norbert Seethaler, Salzburg.

8. Photo Collection of the Kalmbach Publishing Company.

9, 27, 44, 50, 57, 59, 68, 69, 73, 83, 84, 85, 95, 97. Author

10, 40, 87, 88, 89, 99, 100, 101. Michael Robinson, London.

11. Collegiate Church of the Holy Trinity Stratford-upon-Avon, UK.

13. V. Egorov/Tass.

14, 16. Michael Sobolik/Sobolik Studios.

29. Cleveland Museum of Art, purchase from the J. H. Wade Fund 30, 331.

34. Danilo Krstanović, Reuters.

35. Bligh Bond, *Glastonbury Abbey*, 1909.

38. Ezro Stoller/ESTO Photo.

42, 53. David Pereya.

46. Trustees of the Roman Catholic Archdiocese of Liverpool, UK.

49. Henry Kalen Collection, PC 219, University of Manitoba Archive.

56. Norman McGrath Photographer.

60, 61. Richard Rayward, Air Safari Tours, New Zealand.

63, 64. Mark Fram.

71. Parrocchia di Sant'Agnese fuori le Mura, Rome.

72. Commonwealth War Graves Commission, UK.

76. Abbey of Gethsemani Archives, Trappist, KY.

77, 79. ©Milo Keller / www.milokeller.com

91, 92. Cristoph Pfau / Der Oberstadtdirektor, Stadt Bottrop, Germany.

94. The Salvation Army Canada and Bermuda Territory, *The War Cry*

# Appendix A
## A Key to Cross References

After much reflection I have chosen to create new titles for some to the Six Plans listed by Cynthia Harris in her 1958 translation *(The Church Incarnate)* of Rudolf Schwarz's 1938 *Vom Bau der Kirche*. A dualism between Heaven and Earth is threaded through much of Schwarz's writings, uniting such concepts as open and closed, light and dark, arriving and departing. This is of profound scholarly interest, but it could be confusing to those who are setting out to build a church, so I have substituted simple descriptive titles when the relevance of the original titles to the purpose of its Plan could be obscure. A complete listing of the relationships between these titles is set out below

For the First Plan:
"Sacred Inwardness" is substituted for "Sacred Inwardness: The Ring"

For the Second Plan:
"Sacred Meeting" is substituted for "Sacred Parting: The Open Ring"

For the Third Plan:
"The Shining".is substituted for "Sacred Parting: The Chalice of Light"

For the Fourth Plan:
"Sacred Journey" is substituted for "Sacred Journey: The Way"

For the Fifth Plan:
"The Open Chalice" is substituted for "Sacred Cast: The Dark Chalice".

For the Sixth Plan:
"The Dome of Light" is substituted for "Sacred Universe: The Dome of Light.

# Appendix B: Calculation of Reverberation Times

Volume = floor area x average ceiling height
Floor Area = _____ square feet, Average Ceiling Height = _____ feet
Volume V = _____ cubic feet (floor area x height)

| A | B | C | D<br>= BxC | E | F | G<br>= DxF |
|---|---|---|---|---|---|---|
| Element | Length (feet) | Width (feet) | Area | Material | Coeff @ 500 Hz | Absorption (sabins) |
|  |  |  |  |  |  |  |
|  |  |  |  |  |  |  |
|  |  |  |  |  |  |  |
|  |  |  |  |  |  |  |
|  |  |  |  |  |  |  |
|  |  |  |  |  |  |  |
|  |  |  |  |  |  |  |
|  |  |  |  |  |  |  |
|  |  |  |  |  |  |  |
|  |  |  |  |  |  |  |
|  |  |  |  |  |  |  |
| Air | 0.50 x volume / 1,000 ||| | 0.50 |  |
| **Total Absorption for Empty Church (A)** |||||| |
| People | coeff. = 4.00 per person |||| 4.00 |  |
| **Total Absorption with Congregation (A)** |||||| |

Reverberation Time (empty) RT = V / 20A = _____ seconds
Reverberation Time (with .... people) = V / 20A = _____ seconds

# Appendix C

## Sound Absorption Coefficients at 500Hz for various Building Materials (see page 209)

| —CEILINGS— | |
|---|---|
| Gypsum Wallboard (drywall) | 0.07 |
| Plaster | 0.02 |
| Wood Siding | 0.16 |
| Acoustic Tile | 0.65 |

| —WALLS— | |
|---|---|
| Concrete | 0.02 |
| Brick, Painted | 0.02 |
| Brick, Unpainted | 0.04 |
| Concrete Block, Painted | 0.07 |
| Concrete Block, Unpainted | 0.36 |
| Gypsum Wallboard (drywall) | 0.07 |
| Plaster | 0.02 |
| Ceramic Tile, Marble | 0.01 |
| Drapes, Light (hung flat) | 0.16 |
| Drapes Heavy (pleated) | 0.56 |
| Wood Paneling | 0.16 |
| Glass Panels | 0.06 |
| Openings to other rooms | 0.50 |
| Open Doors and Windows | 1.00 |
| Windows for window wall | 0.18 |

| —FLOORS— | |
|---|---|
| Marble | 0.01 |
| Concrete, Terrazzo. Ceramic Tile | 0.02 |
| Tile: Vinyl, Asphalt, Cork, Lino | 0.03 |
| Wood (on Joists) | 0.09 |
| Parquet wood blocks | 0.06 |
| Wood Platform with space below | 0.21 |
| Carpet, glue down | 0.35 |
| Carpet, heavy, on underpad | 0.55 |

| —FURNISHINGS— | |
|---|---|
| Pews per square foot of floor area | 0.20 |
| Pews with Seat Cushions " | 0.45 |
| Chairs (metal or wood) " | 0.05 |
| Chairs, upholstered " | 0.59 |
| Plywood Panels | 0.15 |
| Organ Case, wood | 0.40 |
| Organ Pipes, metal | 0.50 |

| —OCCUPANCY— | |
|---|---|
| People: 4 sabins per person | |
| Air: per 1,000 cubic feet | 2.30 |

# Bibliograhy

Andreae, Johann Valentin. *The Chemical Wedding of Christian Rosencreutz* (1661). Translated by Joscelyn Godwin. Grand Rapids MI: Phanes Press, 1991.

Arthur, Eric. *Toronto, No Mean City*. Oxford University Press, 1964.

Baigent, Michael, Richard Leigh and Henry Lincoln. *Holy Blood and the Holy Grail*. London: Jonathan Cape, 1982.

Billen, Stephanie, *quoted in The Times newspaper* (February 26, 1987). London: The Times, 1987.

Barth, Karl. *Epistle to the Romans*. Translated by E.C. Hoskyns. London: Oxford University Press, 1932.

*The Book of Alternate Services of the Anglican Church of Canada*. Toronto: The Anglican Book Centre, 1985.

Brine, Judith. "The Religious Intentions of the Cambridge Camden Society." *Fabrications: The Journal of the Society of Architectural Historians, Australia and New Zealand*, vol 2, no 1. 1991

Brown, Dan. *Angels and Demons*. New York: Pocket Books, 2000.

Calvin, John. *Ecclesiastical Ordinances* (Geneva 1541). Translated by G. R. Potter and M. Greengrass. London: Arnold, 1983.

Chang, Amos Ih Tioa. *The Tao of Architecture*. Princeton University Press, 1956.

Charles, R. H. *Religious Development between the Old and the New Testaments*. London: Williams and Norgate, 1914.

Cornford, Francis M. *Plato's Cosmology*. New York: Liberal Arts Press, 1957.

Cross, F. L., Editor. *Oxford Dictionary of the Christian Church*, London: Oxford University Press, 1967.

Cyril of Jerusalem. "Mystagogical Catechesis," Translated by E. Yarnold, *Cyril of Jerusalem, The Early Church Fathers*. London: Routledge, 2000.

Dearmer, Percy. *The Parson's Handbook*. London: Humphrey Milford, 1907.

DeWitt, Dennis and Elizabeth. *Modern Architecture in Europe, a Guide to Building since the Industrial Revolution*. London: George Weidenfeld and Nicholson, 1987.

Eco, Umberto. *Foucault's Pendulum*. Translated by William Weaver. San Diego CA: Harcourt Brace Jovanovich, 1989.

Emerson, Ralph Waldo. *Self-Reliance and Other Essays*. New York: Dover, 1975.

Empereur, James. *Models of Liturgical Theology*. Nottingham UK: Grove Books, 1987.

*Evangelical Lutheran Worship*. Minneapolis MN: Augsburg Fortress, 2006.

Foot, Sarah. *Following the Tamar*. Cornwall UK: Bossiney Books, 1980.

Giles, Richard. *Re-pitching the Tent*. Collegeville MN:The Liturgical Press, 1996.

Hooper, John, Bishop of Gloucester. *A Holy Confession* (1547). Cambridge UK: The Parker Society, 1843.

Hughes, Gerard W. *In Search of a Way*. Sydney NSW: E.J. Dwyer Publishers, 1978.

Jasper, R.C. and C. J. Cumming: *Prayers of the Eucharist, Early and Reformed*. New York: Pueblo Publishing, 1987.

Kelty, Matthew. "Gethsemani, Impressions on a Renovation." *Liturgical Arts, vol. 36, No.4*, (August 1968). New York: The Liturgical Arts Society, 1968.

Lao Tzu. *The Tao Te Ching*. Translated by R. L.Wing . New York: Doubleday, 1986.

Levitin, Daniel J. *The World in Six Songs, How the Musical Brain created Human Nature*. Toronto ON: Penguin Canada, 2008.

Lichtenberger, Arthur. *The Day is at Hand*. New York: Seabury Press, 1964.

Mauck, Marchita B. "Ambiguity and Parody". *Liturgy vol. 5, No. 4*, 1986. New York: The Liturgical Society, 1986.

Maurepas, Ginny. "A Place to Loiter." *The Idler,* (May 1988). Toronto: The Idler, 1988.
McArthur, Emily. *Children of Peace.* Toronto: York Pioneer and Historical Society, 1898.
Michell, John. *City of Revelation.* New York: Ballantine Books, 1972.
Moore, Patrick. *Comets.* New York Charles Scribners and Sons, 1985.
Nicholson, Frederick J. "A Hallowed Place." *The Friend,* (March 31 1987). London: The Friend Publications, 1987.
Pierson, Dorothy. "Find a Point of Love." *Daily Word, vol. 127, No 2 (*February 1989). Unity Village, MO: Unity School of Christianity, 1989.
Rauliuk, Nicholas. *A Personal Welcome to the Holy Trinity Cathedral.* Winnipeg MB: Trident Press, 1978.
Reid, Robert L. *Commentary on the Documents of Vatican II.* Edited by Herbert Vorgrimler. New York: Herder and Herder, 1967.
Robinson, Gerald. *Sacred Journey, a Companion to Rudolf Schwarz's "The Church Incarnate".* Eugene OR: Wipf & Stock, 2019.
——— *Theology for Atheists.* Eugene OR: Wipf & Stock, 2019.
Ryan, Maxwell F. "A New Holiness Chorus." *The War Cry,* (October 31, 1987). Toronto: The Salvation Army Canada and Bermuda Territory, 1987.
Schrauwers, Albert. "The Politics of Schism." *Ontario History, vol LXXX No. 1,* (March 1988). Ottawa ON: Canadian Friends Historical Association, 1990.
Schwarz, Rudolf. *The Church Incarnate.* Chicago: Henry Regnery, 1958. Translation by Cynthia Harris of *Vom Bau der Kirche.* Heidelberg: Verlag Lambert Schneider, 1938.
Sitte, Camillo. *Der Stadtbau,* 1889. Translated by George and Christine Collins. Columbia University Studies, Random House, 1965.
Sovik, E.A. *Architecture for Worship.* Minneapolis MN: Augsburg Publications, 1973.
Spencer-Brown, G. *Laws of Form.* London: Allen & Unwin, 1969.
TIME. "An Early Christian Altar." *Time Magazine,* (August 7, 1944). Chicago: Time Inc., 1944.
Trinity Divinity Associates. "Sacred Space and Human Needs". *Prospectus for the Trinity College Divinity Conference,* (June 1988). Toronto: Trinity College, 1988.
Underhill, Evelyn. *Mixed Pasture.* London: Methuen, 1933.
Villette, Jean. *Le Plan de la Cathédral de Chartres, Hasard ou Stricte Géométrie?* Chartres, FR: Les Editions Houvet, 1953.
Visser, Margaret. The Geometry of Love: Space, Time, Mystery and Meaning in an Ordinary Church. Toronto: Harper Flamingo Canada/ Farrar, Strauss and Giroux, 2001.
Vitruvius (Marcus Vitruvius Pollio). "de Architetura, Book 5". Translated by Morris Hicky Morgan, *The Ten Books on Architecture.* London: Oxford University Press, 1914.
von Simson, O. *The Gothic Cathedral.* Princeton NJ: Princeton University Press, 1964.
Ward, W. G. *The Ideal of a Christian Church.* London: James Toovey, 1846.
Weil, Simone. *Waiting on God.* London: Routledge Kegan Paul, 1953.
Whitehead, Alfred North. *Process and Reality: an Essay in Cosmology* (1929). Edited by Griffen and Sherburne. New York: The Free Press, 1979.
William of Malmesbury. *Chronicles of the Kings of England* (1180). Edited by J.A. Giles. Edinburgh: George Bell, 1883.
Williams, H. C. N. *Coventry Cathedral.* Andover, UK: Pitkin Publications, 1971.
Willson, David. *A Collection of Items from the Life of David Willson.* Newmarket ON: G. S. Porter, 1852.
——— *A Short Word to Visitors to the Sharon Temple,* Toronto: York Pioneer and Historical Society, 1831.
Yarnold, E. *Cyril of Jerusalem, The Early Church Fathers.* London: Routledge, 2000

# Index

## A

acoustics, 208
Allward, Walter, 139
*Architecture for Worship*, 27
Atheism, 218
Augustine of Hippo, 6, 215

## B

Baigent, Michael, 79
baptism, 217–221
basilicas, 199
Boniface IV, Pope, 125
Brasilia, 15

## C

Calvin, John, 188
Camden Society, 201
Cathedral of All Times, 8
CERN, 19
Chang, Amos Ih Tioa, 13
choirs, 35, 206, 213
Churches
    All Saints, Toronto, 98
    Assumption, Sarajevo, 71
    Basilian Chapel, Toronto, 103
    Bloordale United, Toronto, 85
    Christ the King, Liverpool, 87
    Coventry Cathedral, 152, 159
    Saint-Loup Diaconesses, 146
    Gethsemani Abbey, 143, 202
    Glastonbury Mary Chapel, 73
    Good Shepherd, Tepako, 114
    Holy Trinity, Stratford, 23
    Holy Trinity, Toronto, 17, 177, 205
    Heilig-Kreuz, Bottrop, 166
    KwaMashu Meeting, 175
    Lourdes Basilica Pius X, 21
    Notre Dame de France, London, 77
    Pantheon, Rome, 125
    St. Agnes, Rome, 132
    St. Andrew's, Toronto, 127
    St. George the Martyr, Toronto, 154
    St. James's Piccadilly, 181
    St. John Evangelist, Ottawa, 203
    St. John's, Kanata, 220
    St. Mark's, Burlington, Vermont, 77
    St. Mary Magdalene, Picton, 192
    St. Peter's, Manhattan, 107, 127
    St. Thomas's, St. Catharines, 110
    Trinity College Chapel, 140, 202
    Trinity, Charles City, 28
    Winnipeg Orthodox Cathedral, 94
    Wycliffe Chapel, Toronto, 82
Churchill, Winston S, 3
Citicorp Center, Manhattan, 107
city, the, 14–18, 113, 180–185
*City of God*, 6
city planning, 14
Cocteau, Jean, 80
Coffee Hour, 190
confirmation, 217
Confucius, 6
Contemplation,
    see Ministries
Cormier, Ernest, 102
Cranmer, Thomas, 202
Cycle of Nature, 10
Cycle of Worship, 35, 38, 41–52, 61–84, 194
Cyril of Jerusalem, 124

## D

Dearmer, Percy, 135
Dedication,
    see Ministries
*Der Stadtbau*, 14, 16
Dome of Darkness, 123–130
Dome of Light,
    see Six Plans

## E

Eco, Umberto, 33
Eilers, Fr. Wilhelm, 1676
Emerson, Ralph Waldo, 61
Empereur, James, 53–56
Endsleigh Estate, 30
Eucharist, 68–70, 85, 106, 131
  142, 172–185, 198–218
Euclid, 52
Evangelism,
  see Ministries

## F

Fellowship Baptists, 123
Fifth Plan,
  see Six Plans, The
First Plan,
  see Six Plans, The
Fisk, Jim, 205
Fourth Plan,
  see Six Plan, The
Freyssinet, Eugène, 22

## G

Genesis, 7
Gibberd, Sir Frederick, 87
Giles, Reginald, 105
Grand Central Terminal, 20
greeters, 193
growth, 9

## H

Haussmann, Baron, 15
Higgs boson, 19
Hooper, John, Bishop, 92, 200

## I

internet, 146, 190

## J

Jenkins, David, Bishop, 104
John XXIII, Pope, 135
Joseph of Arimathea, 73
Justice, see Ministries

## K

Kelty, Matthew, 145
Kettle, John, 2

## L

Lao Tzu, 13
Last Supper, 68, 76
Laud, William, Archbishop, 92, 200
*Laws of Form*, 18
Lenin's Tomb, 26
Levitin, Daniel J., 58
lighting, 203
Localarchitecture, 146
Luther, Martin, 200
Lutyens, Sir Edwin, 58–60, 87

## M

mandala, 45–50, 65, 119
Mauck, Marchita, 163
Michell, John, 75
Mies van der Rohe, Ludwig, 96
Ministries, Six, 34, 63–64
  Contemplation, 34–38, 45–50, 60,
    68, 71, 83
  Pastoral Care, 34–51, 90, 112, 162,
    193
  Witness, 34–39, 45–59, 105–122,
    128, 153, 194
  Dedication, 34–39, 48–55, 131–148,
    194
  Evangelism, 35–40, 45–50, 120,
    151–158, 120, 194
  Justice, 35–37, 40, 45–50, 60, 171–
    185, 194
models, 53–56
monasteries, 143–145, 200–201
music, 99, 206–214

## O

O'Driscoll, Herbert 64
Open Chalice,
  see Six Plans
organ, 206–208, 216
Orthodox Communion, 94–97

Our Father, 36–42, 51–53

## P

Page and Steele, 127
parameters, 32–36, 45, 50–56, 103, 122, 173, 194
Pastoral Care,
    see Ministries
Pentecostals, 49. 121
perfect numbers, 6
Philip, Apostle, 73
Plans,
    see the Six Plans
plants, 9
Plato, 52, 60
preaching, 213
Priory of Zion, 79
process theology, 55
processions, 214–215, 221

## Q

Quakers, 117

## R

Ring of Plans, 9, 53, 57, 67, 83
Robinson, Gerald, 2, 110, 153, 186

## S

Sabine, Charles Wallace, 208
Sacred Inwardness,
    see Six Plans
Sacred Journey,
    see Six Plans
Sacred Meeting,
    see Six Plans
sacred space, 25–27, 29–31
Salvation Army, 175
Salzburg, 16
Sarajevo, 71
Schwarz, Rudolf, 1, 7–11, 37, 53, 61, 64–66, 149, 166, 192–196
Scott, Sir Giles Gilbert, 140, 159
scripture, 32, 206
seating, 78, 97, 113, 145, 186, 202
secondary ministries, 41–50

Seventh Plan, The, 7–8
*Shaping Space for Worship*, 58, 60, 221
Shickel, William, 143
Shining, The,
    see Six Plans
Shiva Nataraja, 57
singing, 206, 214
Sitte, Camillo, 14, 17, 18
Six Plans, The, 1–11, 32, 51, 53, 61–65, 106, 166
The First Plan,
    Sacred Inwardness,4, 11, 45, 70–89, 102
The Second Plan,
    Sacred Meeting, 4, 7, 11, 34, 48, 90–104, 193
The Third Plan,
    The Shining, 4, 11, 48, 105–122, 134
The Fourth Plan,
    Sacred Journey, 5, 11, 45 131–149, 202,
The Fifth Plan,
    The Open Chalice, 5, 11, 45, 151–170
The Sixth Plan,
    The Dome of Light, 5–11, 171–185
Society of Friends, 25, 117
songs, 58
Sovik, Edward, 27
space, 2, 3, 12–14, 17, 18, 31, 61, 64, 186, 197, 199, 201
Spence, Sir Basil, 159
Spencer-Brown, George, 18
sphere, 52
Stalin, Josef, 26
Stevenson, Kenneth, 220
Stratford, 25
Stubbins, Hugh, 105–109

## T

*The Tao of Architecture*, 13
*The Tao of Power*, 13
Third Plan,
    see Six Plans, The
*TIME magazine*, 77, 202

Trappists, 143
Trinity College, 202

## U

Underhill, Evelyn, 30
United Church, 29, 85, 127–130
Unity Church, 25

## V

Vatican II, 77, 135, 167
Venerable Bede, 125
Vimy, 139

## W

War Memorial, Vimy, France, 139
Ward, W.G., 100
Weil, Simone, 36, 38, 42, 57
Whitehead, Alfred North, 55
William of Malmesbury, 73
Willson, David, 118, 121
Witness, see Ministries
*World in Six Songs*, 58
Worship, 6. 10. 22, 27, 30–50' 51, 61–64, 76, 186, 189,
Wren, Sir Christopher, 63, 180

www.ingramcontent.com/pod-product-compliance
Lightning Source LLC
Chambersburg PA
CBHW062019220426
43662CB00010B/1399